Ribbonwork

Ribbonwork

HILARY EVANS

BOBBS-MERRILL INDIANAPOLIS/NEW YORK

to my parents

Copyright © 1976 Hilary Evans

All rights reserved. No part of this publication
may be reproduced, stored in a retrieval system,
or transmitted in any form or by any means, electronic,
mechanical, photocopying, recording or otherwise,
without the prior permission of the publisher.

First published in the USA 1976 by
The Bobbs-Merrill Company, Inc.
Indianapolis   New York

Produced by Walter Parrish International Limited, London
Drawings by the author
Photographs taken by Gordon Roberton of A C Cooper Limited, London

Printed and bound in Great Britain by Purnell & Sons Limited

Contents

Introduction 6
Ribbon borders 8
Wall hanging 13
Table-mats 16
Desk set 18
Bookmarks 20
Hair ribbons 26
Roses 30
Tank top 35
Fringes 37
Velvet cushion cover 42
Peg dolls 45
Belts 49
Abstract picture 53
Aprons 57
Child's bolero 68
Embroidered box 72
Drawstring bag 75
Drawn-thread tablecloth 78
Baby's angel top 81
Woven cushion 86
Dried flowers 90
Macramé hanging 99
Patchwork cover 102
Shopping bag 106

Metric conversion table 111

Introduction

Ribbons are a wonderfully versatile and rewarding medium to work in, mainly due to the multitude of different kinds sold over the country—satin, rayon, nylon, velvet, woven and printed patterns, braids and ric-rac, cotton tapes, lace and eyelet (broderie anglaise), and motif ribbons. There is also great variation in the widths (anything from $\frac{1}{4}$ inch to 4 inches) and a positive rainbow of colours, particularly in velvet. With a little imagination and inventiveness, the uses of ribbon, both practical and decorative, are infinite. It should be thought of as a material as well as a decoration, for it can be used as a fabric in appliqués and woven work, or as a thread in knitting and crocheting.

From the time that pedlars went their rounds with trimmings and laces and bright shiny beads, ribbon has been used extensively for adorning clothes and personal belongings, for braiding curlers, for looping around baskets, embroidering on quilts, and so on. During Victorian times especially, women's dresses and hats were elaborately trimmed with yards of the stuff, woven in intricate designs, and European peasant costumes have always been decorated with brightly-coloured patterned braids. Nowadays, as before, there is no need to stop at clothes—almost everything worn or used can be gaily decorated.

All the materials required are fairly simple and can easily be bought in local shops and department stores. No special knowledge of any handicraft is necessary, other than a basic understanding of sewing and the rudiments of knitting (for the tank top) and crochet (for the drawstring bag), as detailed step-by-step instructions are given for each project. In fact several of the items could easily be made by children. It is worth noting that some of the measurements given for the large amounts of ribbon are, by nature, slightly variable and so should not be taken absolutely literally. Similarly the colours given are merely examples—other schemes should be experimented with as much as possible. In order to avoid repetition it has been assumed that certain basic materials are always at hand, such as pins, needles, tacking thread, sewing cotton, scissors, and a tape measure. Although a sewing machine is not essential, it would obviously make some of the longer and more complicated articles much easier and faster. To help the reader the materials are listed in the order that they are used, the diagrams are numbered with the text instruction number for easy identification, and a metric conversion table is included at the back. Remember to bear in mind that washable and colourfast ribbons should be used for certain of the items.

It is greatly hoped that you will not only find these projects satisfying and enormous fun to do, but also that you will be stimulated to adapt and develop the ideas further, for there is so much that can be made and so many new and exciting ways in which ribbonwork can become a craft, an art, and a resource.

Ribbon borders

Borders usually consist of straight lines of ribbon or ric-rac braid, too much of which can be rather dull. This sampler illustrates how variety and movement can be introduced by gathering, folding, or pleating. It is 24" by 18" in size.

Materials
Lengths of ribbon ranging in width from ¼" to 1", in any colours
White cotton or linen backing material

Gathering
An amount of ribbon twice the length of the finished frill is required for all four of the gathered borders illustrated.

1 The first border is made by making two parallel rows of small running stitch close together at the top edge of the ribbon. Mark the ribbon every 8" with a pin and the backing material every 4"—these marks will be aligned to ensure that the gathers are evenly spaced. Draw up the gathering threads so that the ribbon is half its original length and align the marker pins. Pin the frill onto the backing material and tack and machine stitch it in place along the top. The holding pins can be left while machining, provided they are in a vertical position, as they help to keep the gathers down. Remove the pins and the tacking and gathering stitches.

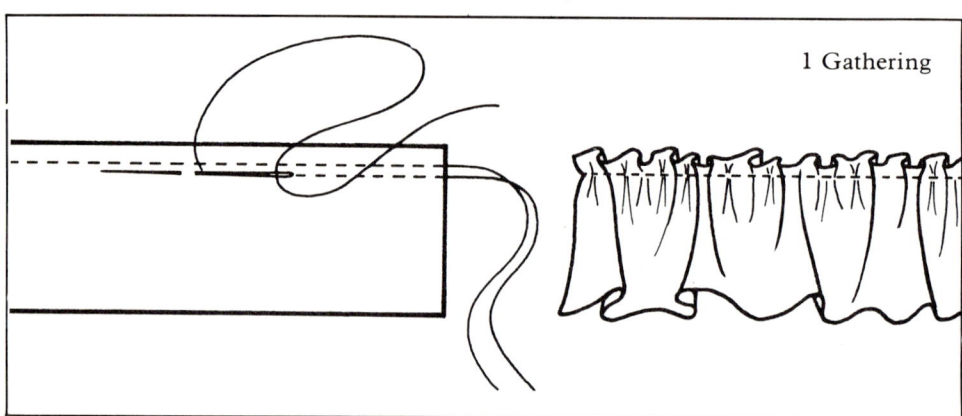

1 Gathering

2 The next frill is rather complicated to make but looks very effective, especially if ribbon narrower than ½" is used. Place marker pins at 1" intervals along the ribbon. Leaving the first 1" section free, make a central row of small running stitches in the second 1" section. Draw the thread up tightly to make a tiny rosette and fasten at the back of the

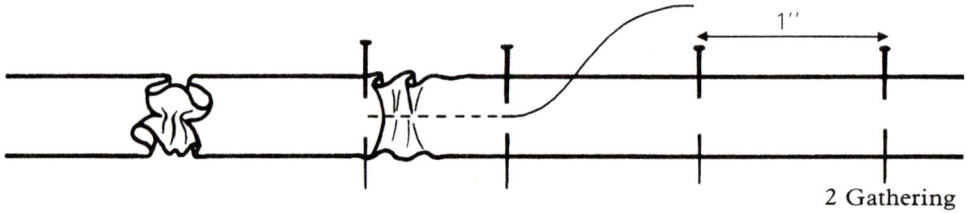

2 Gathering

Borders

2 Gathering

ribbon. Gather every alternate 1" section, removing the marker pins as each rosette is completed. Pin and tack the ribbon onto the backing material, and stitch it in place by hand with tiny running or back stitches down the centre.

3 The third ribbon on the sampler is a variation of the first method of gathering. This time make two rows of running stitch down the centre of the ribbon. Gather up and machine stitch the ribbon down the centre.

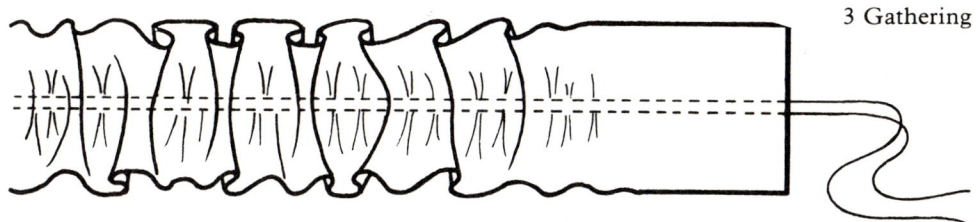

3 Gathering

4 Another way to gather ribbon is diagonally to produce a wave-like effect. Place marker pins alternately at either edge of the ribbon at intervals equal to twice the width of the ribbon, as shown. Working across the ribbon from pin to pin, make two diagonal rows of running stitch. Draw them up so that the stitching makes one straight line, and secure the gathered ribbon onto the backing material with tacking and machine stitching as described above.

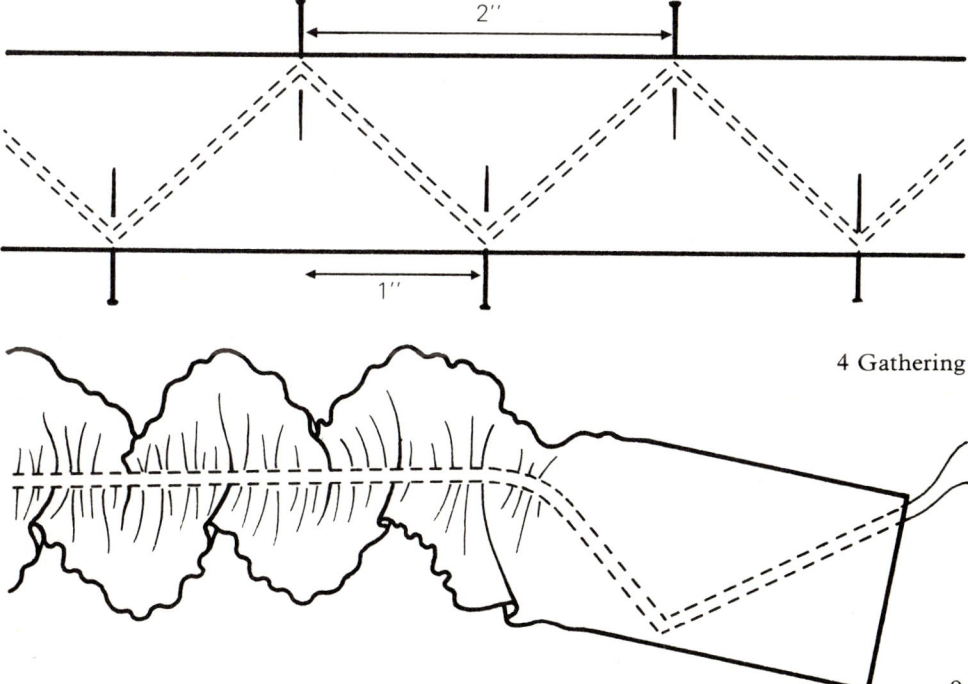

4 Gathering

Borders

Folding
The following four borders were made by folding the ribbon in various ways. The diagonal folds require ribbon about twice the finished length of the border.

1 To ensure that the diagonals in the first border remain constant, make guide lines of two parallel rows of tacking stitch the depth of the finished border on the backing material, and mark with pins the places where the points of the diagonals are to occur, making sure they are equidistant. Then simply pin the ribbon onto the backing material, folding it over at every marker pin. Tack and sew it into place with a single central row of stitches. If the ribbon is wider than $\frac{1}{2}''$ make a row of stitches along each edge.

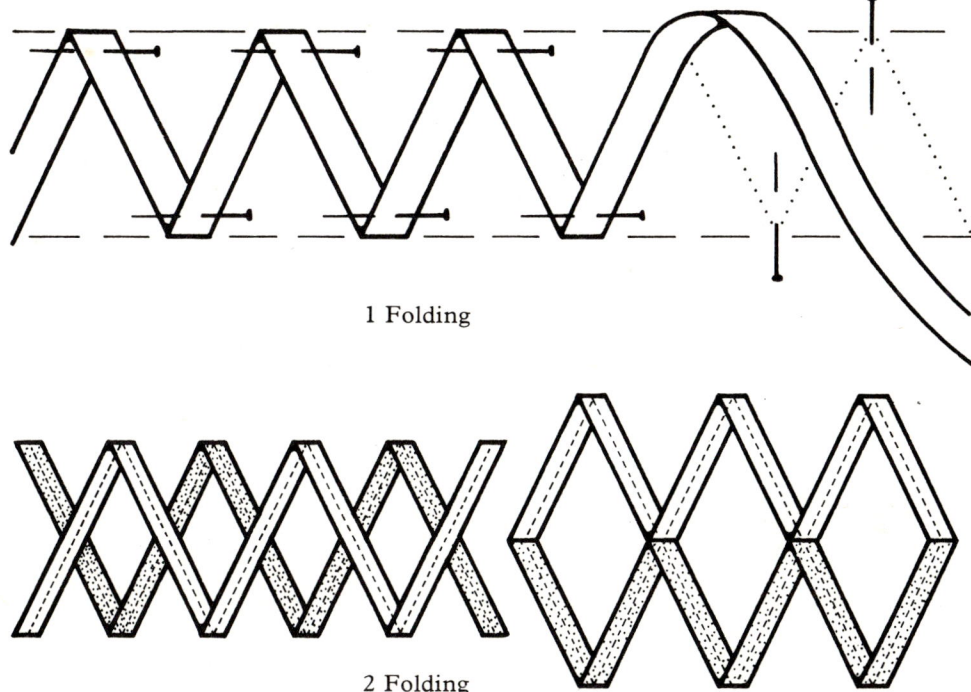

1 Folding

2 Folding

2 By using more than one row of diagonally folded ribbon, more complex patterns can be made. If one length of ribbon is used over another, stitch the lower one down first.

3 Turret shapes are made by folding the ribbon vertically and horizontally. As with the diagonally folded ribbons, guide lines of tacking stitch should first be worked on the backing material. The shape of the turret

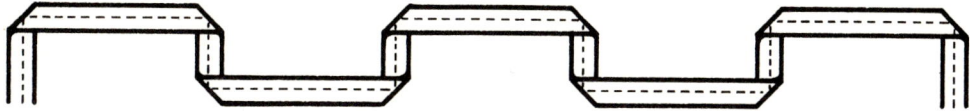

3 Folding

11

Borders

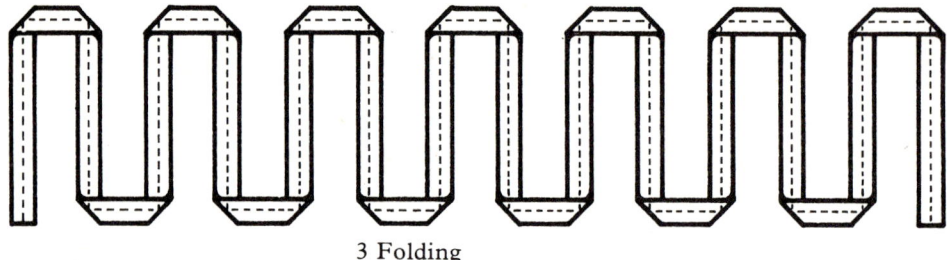

3 Folding

is controlled by varying the width and height. For example, the illustrated border has long horizontals and short verticals but if these lengths are reversed, a very different pattern occurs.

4 The last border is a variation on the first zigzag border. Proceed as before, but here loop the ribbon over at the point of each diagonal.

4 Folding

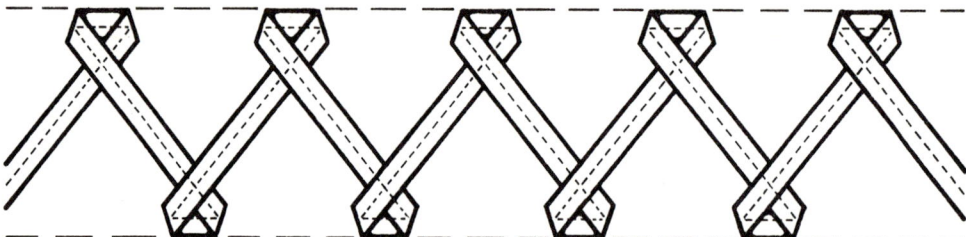

Pleating
The main point to remember when pleating ribbons is that all the pleats must be of equal size to achieve the formal appearance required. The three borders illustrated show how different results are obtained by varying the direction of the pleat.

1 The amount of ribbon required for the first border is two and a half times the finished length. Make pleats of any chosen size alternately above and below the ribbon, leaving a space the width of a pleat between each fold. Hold them in place with pins and then tacking stitch, and finally secure the border with a central row of machine stitching.

1 Pleating

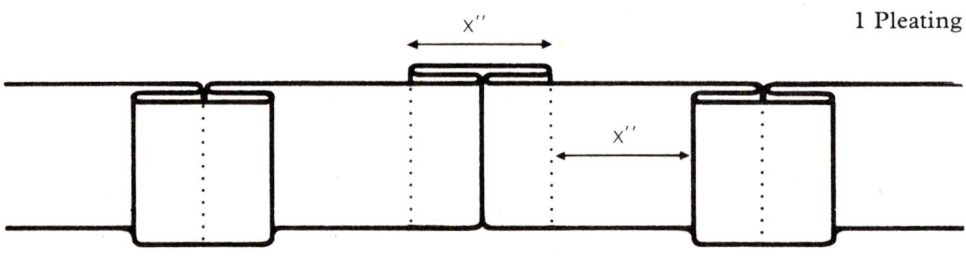

12

Wall hanging

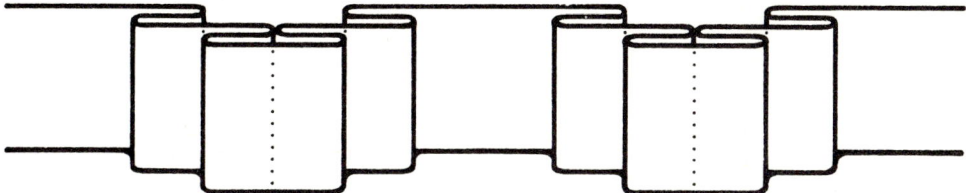

2   A variation on the above is to make groups of two left-facing and two right-facing pleats, with short lengths of ribbon between each group. Stitch the border onto the background material with a central row of machine stitching. Ribbon two and a half times the length of the finished border will be needed.

3   The final border is the simplest to make as all the pleats are folded in the same direction. Three times the border-length of ribbon is required, and again it is secured by a central row of machine stitching.

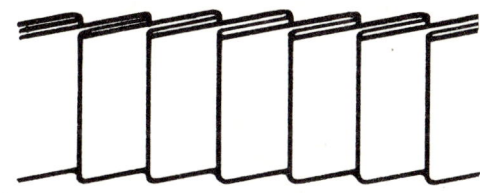

Wall hanging

A free-form wall hanging is easily made by weaving ribbons of different widths and textures in lines and blocks to form an all-over pattern. It is advisable to first make a rough plan with pencil and paper of the pattern to be woven. The hanging illustrated is $13\frac{1}{2}''$ by $31''$.

Materials
36 yards ribbon $\frac{3}{8}''$ wide in base colour
2 wooden rods 18″ long (about $\frac{3}{8}''$ diameter)
20 yards of various toning ribbons in differing lengths and widths

1   Cut 19 pieces of ribbon 33″ long in base colour for warp (lengthwise) threads. Fold all the ends over 1″ and stitch down to make loops to hold the rods at both ends.

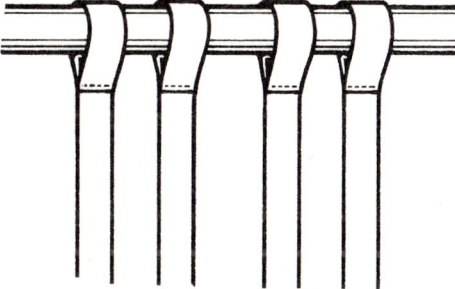

1 Wall hanging

2   Slip the rods through the loops and arrange the warp threads regularly or freely, grouping the ribbons in twos and threes and leaving suitable spaces between them. Do not make the spaces larger than 3″ or the weft (cross) ribbons will sag.

13

Wall hanging

3 Tightly sew a 24" length of narrow ribbon to the top rod, on either side of the warp threads. Hang the 'skeleton' wall hanging up by this ribbon at a convenient height for weaving (about shoulder level). Obviously the height will have to be altered as the work progresses.

4 It is best to start and finish with several complete lines of cross threads as this helps to hold the hanging together. Starting at the top, weave the first weft ribbons. As each section is finished, pin the ribbons in place at either side and also secure them in the middle to several warp threads. Obviously

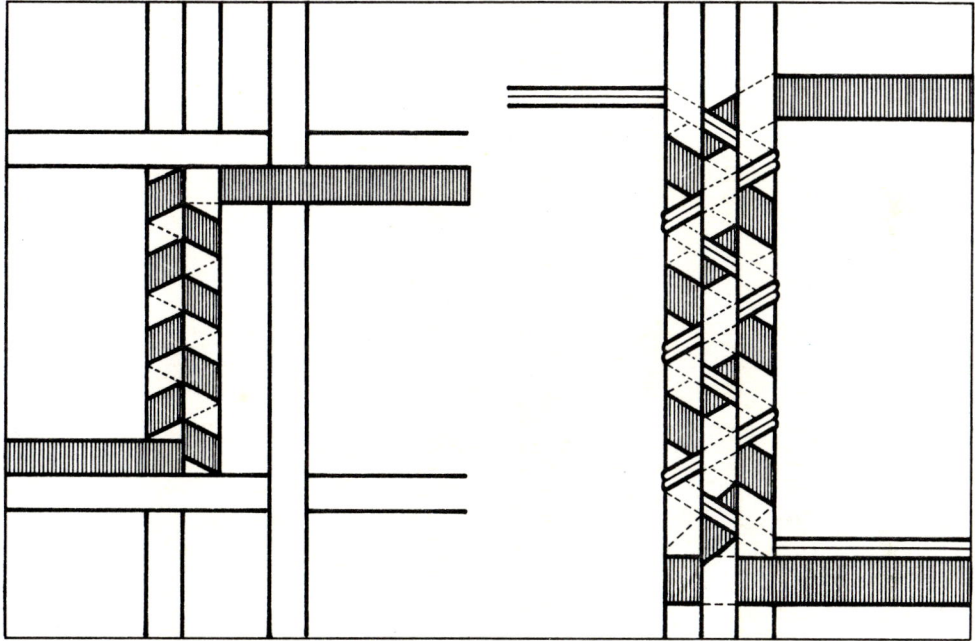

5 Wall hanging

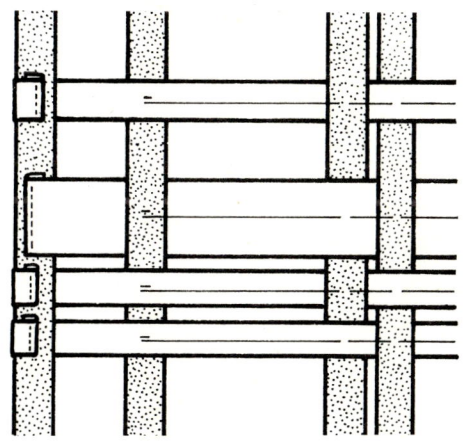

6 Wall hanging

the lengths of the weft ribbons will vary according to how they are woven.

5 Make points of interest in the hanging by experimenting with different weaving patterns as shown.

6 When the weaving is completed turn the hanging over to the wrong side. Trim the weft ribbons at the edges, turn under $\frac{1}{4}$", and sew them to the warp threads. Catch the weft threads with tiny stitches to hold them in place and prevent them sagging.

7 Carefully press the hanging with a cool iron.

15

Table-mats

Petersham or grosgrain ribbon is very serviceable and therefore extremely suitable for decorating table-mats. The ones described here are simply designed and easy to make.

Materials
$\frac{3}{4}$ yard beige heavy-weight cotton, linen, or any firm washable material 36" or 45" wide
7 yards beige or white tape $\frac{1}{2}$" wide
3 lengths of petersham or grosgrain ribbon, $2\frac{1}{4}$ yards long and $\frac{5}{8}$" wide in maroon, yellow, and cerise

1 Cut four pieces of beige cotton, linen, or washable material $17\frac{1}{2}$" by 13" for the mats. Fold the raw edges under $\frac{1}{4}$" (onto the wrong side) and tack down.

2 Pin beige or white tape over these raw edges, mitre each corner (tuck the tape under so that the fold is diagonal), and tack into place. Machine stitch the tape onto the material with a row of stitches along each edge. Remove all tacking.

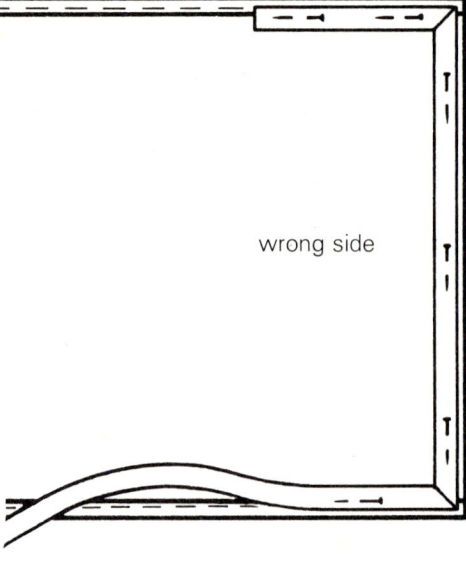

2 Table-mats

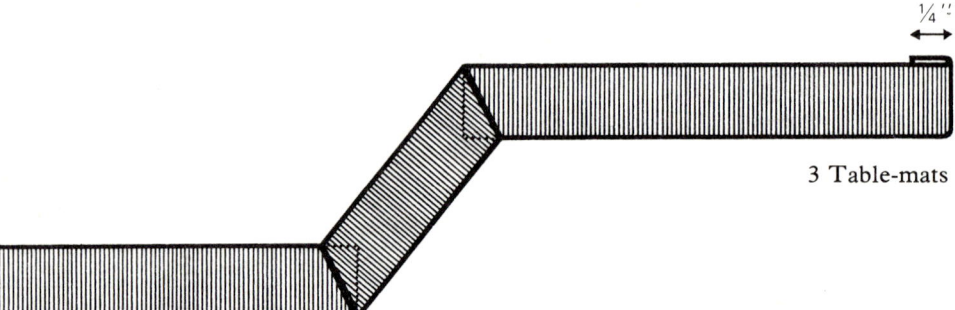

3 Table-mats

3 Cut each length of the coloured ribbon into four. Take a piece of maroon ribbon and turn the end under $\frac{1}{4}$". Pin it onto the left-hand side of one of the mats, $1\frac{3}{4}$" from and parallel to the top edge. Follow the diagram for the diagonal folds, making a right over left fold first and then a left over right fold. Pin the rest of the ribbon along the right half of the top edge of the mat, turning the right-hand end under $\frac{1}{4}$". Tack in place.

4 Pin and tack the yellow ribbon directly under the maroon one, following the outline exactly, and similarly pin and tack the cerise

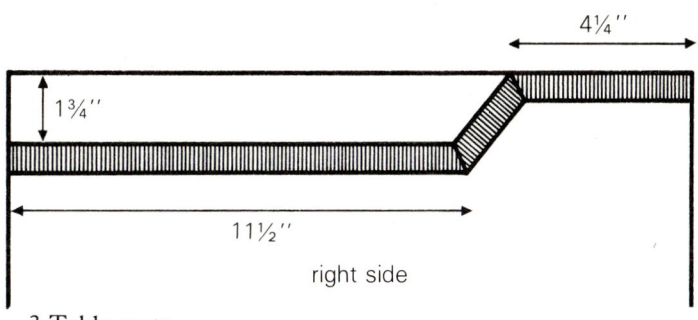

3 Table-mats

ribbon under the yellow one. Neaten all the raw ends by turning them under $\frac{1}{4}''$. The order of the strips can be altered or reversed on the other mats but on a light coloured background it is more effective to keep a light tone between two dark ones.

5 Complete the pinning and tacking of the ribbons on all four mats before machining them down — this saves continually changing the cotton in the sewing machine. Remember to keep the stitching very close to the edge of the ribbons.

6 Remove all tacking and press the mats on the wrong side.

17

Desk set

Whether in the home, office, or school, a desk set is always very useful. The cans and blotter are covered in flocked, self-adhesive plastic and trimmed with tartan ribbon. Coloured paper could be used instead of plastic, and boxes instead of cans. As it is very easy, this is a good project for children.

Materials
2 cans about 3″ and 4″ high (one with a lid)
¾ yard red self-adhesive plastic 18″ wide
2 yards tartan ribbon 1″ wide
Clear adhesive
Cardboard 12″ by 18″
Thin cardboard 5″ by 9″

The cans

1 Find two clean cans, a small one with a lid for storing paperclips, drawing pins, etc, and a larger one for holding pens, pencils, or paintbrushes.

2 Cut two rectangles of self-adhesive plastic to cover the sides of the two cans, allowing an extra ¼″ in the circumference for an overlap. Also cover the lid of the smaller one with plastic.

3 Cut pieces of tartan ribbon the length of the circumference of the cans plus ¾″ to allow for a ¼″ turn under and a ½″ overlap to prevent fraying. Trim the top and bottom of the cans by gluing the ribbon in position.

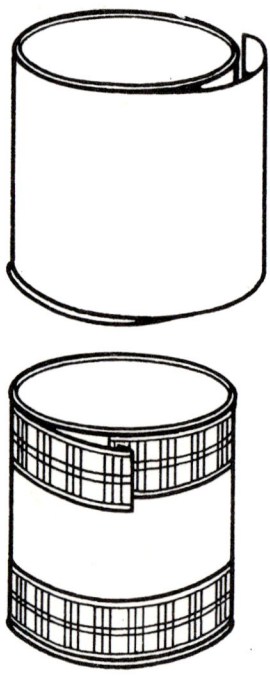

The blotter

1 Cut two rectangles of cardboard, one 8¾″ by 11¼″ and the other, which forms the base of the blotter, 9″ by 11½″. Then cut two rectangles of self-adhesive plastic 10¾″ by 13¼″ and 11″ by 13½″.

2 Cover the cardboard pieces with the plastic, trim the corners as shown, and fold the edges over onto the back.

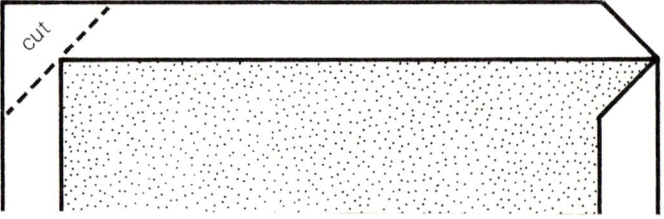

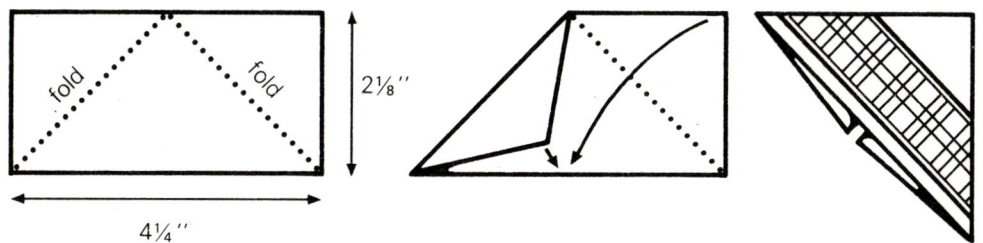

3 Make the corner pieces that hold the sheets of blotting paper from four pieces of thin cardboard $4\frac{1}{4}''$ by $2\frac{1}{8}''$. Cover one side of each with self-adhesive plastic. With plastic side down, fold them into triangles as shown. Decorate by gluing on a piece of tartan ribbon, keeping the ends out of sight at the back of the triangle.

4 Glue the four trimmed triangular pieces over each corner of the smaller covered rectangle (at the base only). Finally glue the blotter centrally onto the covered cardboard base, so that there is an $\frac{1}{8}''$ border all round.

Bookmarks

Making bookmarks is an effective way of using up any odd remnants of ribbon or braid. It is best to use thin card or cardboard, but alternatively thick paper is just as good. A similar method could be used to cover telephone and memo pads.

Design 1

Materials
Thin white card $6\frac{1}{2}''$ by $2''$
$\frac{1}{2}$ yard of wide ric-rac braid
$\frac{1}{4}$ yard fancy braid $\frac{3}{4}''$ wide
Clear adhesive

1 Measure and cut a piece of thin card $6\frac{1}{2}''$ long and $2''$ wide. Round off the corners by placing a small circular object such as a button or coin about $1''$ in diameter at each corner and draw round it in pencil. Cut along the pencil line.

2 Cut two pieces of ric-rac braid $8\frac{1}{2}''$ long and using a clear adhesive, glue them symmetrically in place on the card. Ease the ends of the braid together and join them with a few small stitches to form a loop at each end of the bookmark.

3 Cut a piece of fancy braid $6\frac{1}{2}''$ long. Turn under the raw ends and glue this on top of the ric-rac.

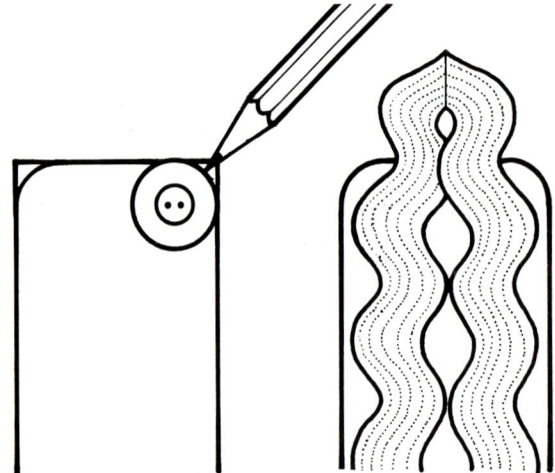

Design 2

Materials
Thin coloured card $7''$ by $3\frac{1}{2}''$
$\frac{1}{4}$ yard braid $1\frac{1}{4}''$ wide
Clear adhesive
Hole-punch
$\frac{1}{2}$ yard ribbon $\frac{3}{8}''$ wide

1 Cut a piece of thin coloured card $7''$ long and $3\frac{1}{2}''$ wide. With the right side up, score a line down the centre. In the right half make two horizontal cuts of $1\frac{1}{4}''$ (the same width as the braid), one $\frac{1}{2}''$ from the top and the other $\frac{3}{4}''$ from the bottom of the card. These cuts must be equidistant from each side.

Bookmarks

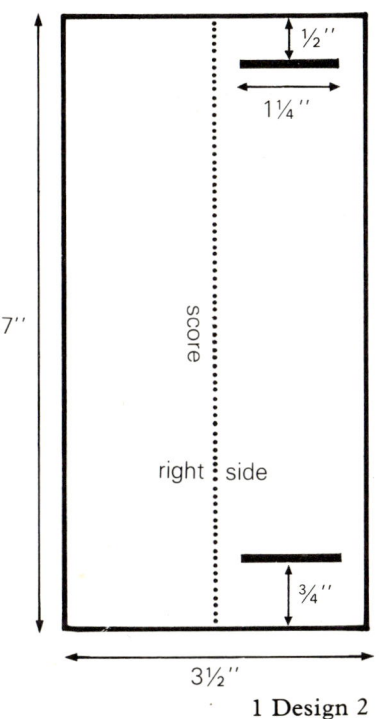

1 Design 2

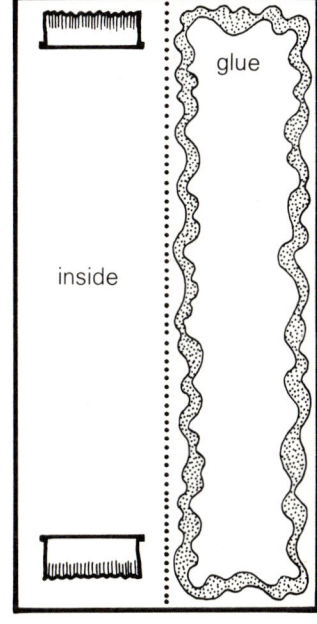

2 Design 2

2 Lay the braid down the right half of the card, slip the ends through the cuts to the back, and fix in place with clear adhesive. Then glue the inside edges of the card and fold it in half along the scored line, pressing the two sides firmly together.

3 With a hole-punch make three holes across the bottom of the bookmark, $\frac{1}{4}''$ apart and $\frac{1}{4}''$ up from the edge.

4 Measure three 6" lengths of ribbon and cut a V shape into each end to prevent fraying. Fold these pieces in half and thread the looped ends through the punched holes from the back of the bookmark. Slip the ends through the loops and draw up firmly.

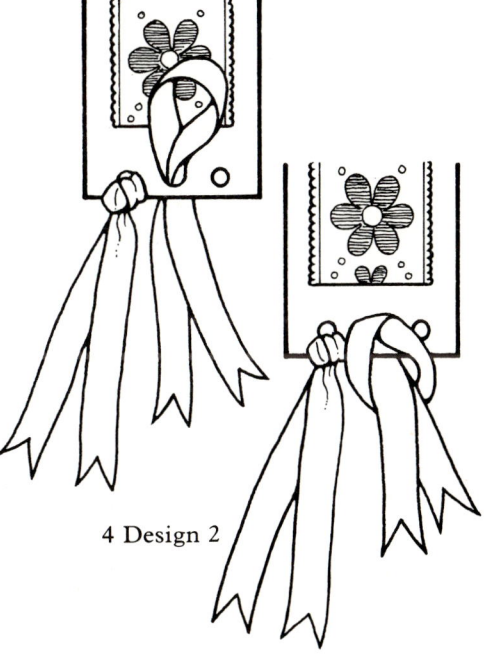

4 Design 2

Design 3

Materials
Thin coloured card 7" by 4"
5 lengths of ribbon $\frac{3}{8}$" wide and 15" long in red, orange, pink, yellow, and green
Clear adhesive
$\frac{1}{2}$ yard floral trimming

1. Using five different coloured ribbons make a $6\frac{1}{2}$" piece of plaiting (braiding) by following the instructions below, and secure each end with a few small running stitches. It may be found to be easier if the ends are pinned down to hold them steady while working.
fold red over orange under pink
fold yellow over green under red
fold orange over pink under yellow
fold green over red under orange
fold pink over yellow under green
fold red over orange under pink
fold yellow over green under red
fold orange over pink under yellow
fold green over red under orange
fold pink over yellow under green

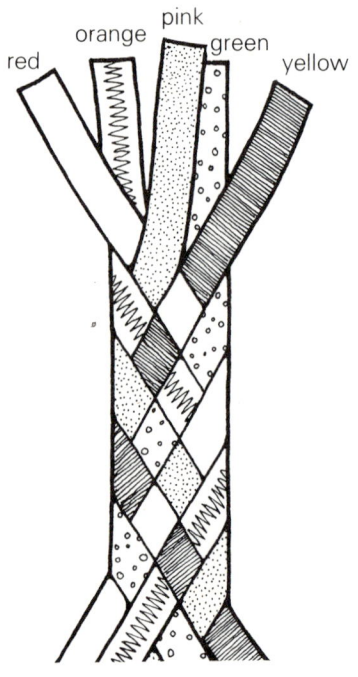

22

Bookmarks

2 Cut a piece of thin coloured card 7" long and 4" wide. With the right side up, score a line down the centre. In the right half make two horizontal cuts the width of the plait, $\frac{1}{2}"$ from the top and bottom edges. Slip the ends of the plait through these cuts to the back and glue in position.

along the inside edges of the card, fold it in half along the scored line, and press the two sides firmly together.

4 Finish the bookmark by surrounding the edge of the plait with floral trimming held in place by clear adhesive.

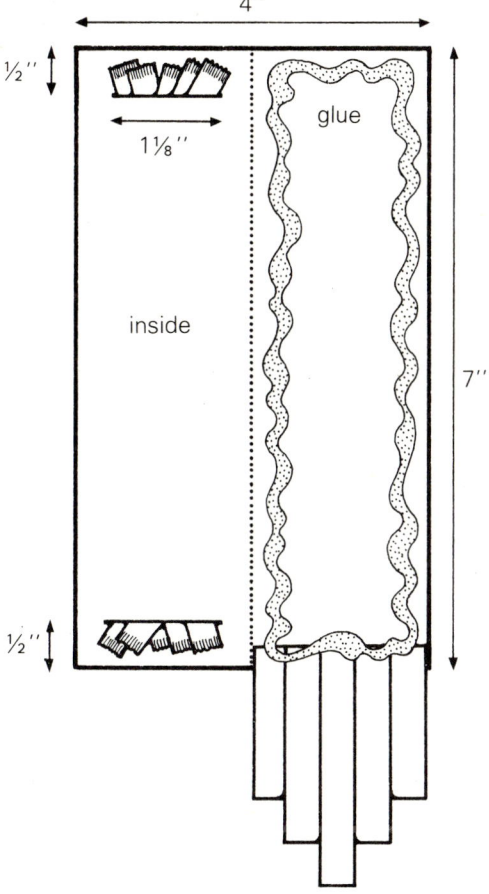

Design 4

If pressed flowers are unobtainable, cut tiny coloured photographs of flowers and plants out of a magazine and make a composite design. In this case there is no need to cover the design with clear plastic material as its only purpose is to protect the dried flowers which tend to be very brittle.

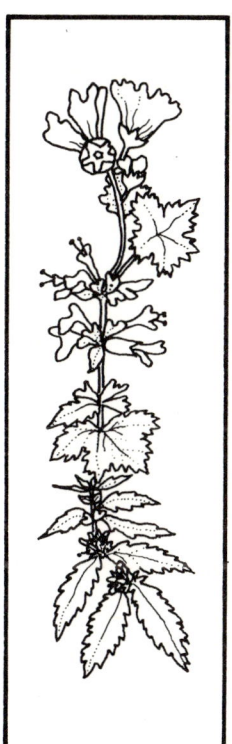 

3 Cut five lengths of ribbon for the fringe as follows: two pieces $3\frac{1}{2}"$ long (pink and orange), two pieces $4\frac{1}{2}"$ long (yellow and green), and one piece $5\frac{1}{2}"$ long (red). Fold the lengths in half and glue the raw ends together and then to the inside right edge of the card. Spread glue

Design 4: using pressed flowers (left) or photographs (right)

Bookmarks

Materials
2 pieces of thin coloured card 7" by 2"
Pressed flowers and leaves
Clear adhesive
Piece of clear, flexible plastic 7" by 2"
$\frac{1}{2}$ yard beige velvet ribbon $\frac{3}{8}$" wide
$\frac{1}{4}$ yard brown velvet ribbon $\frac{3}{8}$" wide
$\frac{1}{4}$ yard satin, rayon, or nylon ribbon $\frac{3}{8}$" wide

1. Cut two pieces of thin coloured card 7" long and 2" wide. Arrange the pressed flowers on one of the pieces and stick them into place with a few spots of clear adhesive along the stalks and under the tips of the leaves and flowers.

2. Cut a piece of clear plastic 7" long and 2" wide. Carefully spread adhesive along the edges of the card and stick the piece of plastic over the flower pattern.

3. Cut two pieces of beige velvet ribbon 7" long and glue them over the clear plastic down each side. Complete the edging by adding two pieces of brown velvet ribbon $2\frac{1}{2}$" long across the top and bottom. Turn the ribbon ends over and stick them to the back of the card and glue the second piece of card over the back to cover the raw ends.

4. Make a small bow of satin, rayon, or nylon ribbon (velvet is too bulky) and glue it to the bottom of the bookmark.

Design 5

Materials
Clear, flexible plastic 7" by $3\frac{3}{4}$"
Hole-punch
Small photographs
Thin coloured card $6\frac{1}{2}$" by $1\frac{1}{2}$"
Clear adhesive
$1\frac{1}{4}$ yards ribbon $\frac{1}{4}$" wide

1. Cut a piece of clear plastic 7" long and $3\frac{3}{4}$" wide and fold it in half lengthwise. Shape one end by trimming the corners as shown.

2. With a hole-punch make one hole at the base, four holes at the top, and twelve holes down each side. There should be a space of $\frac{1}{8}$" between the holes and the edge of the plastic.

3. Select some photographs of suitable size and trim them to $1\frac{1}{2}$" wide. Cut a piece of thin coloured card $6\frac{1}{2}$" long and $1\frac{1}{2}$" wide, trim to a point at the base, and glue the photographs to one side (alternatively they could be stuck to both sides). Slip the piece of card between the two halves of the folded plastic.

4. From the back of the bookmark draw 1 yard of ribbon through the

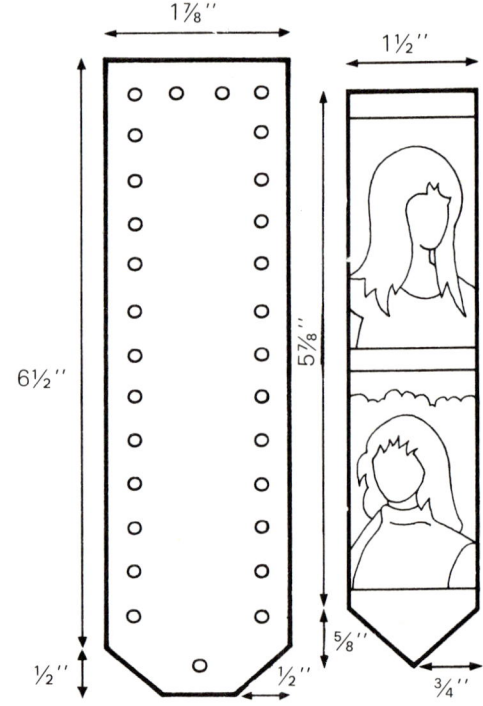

Bookmarks

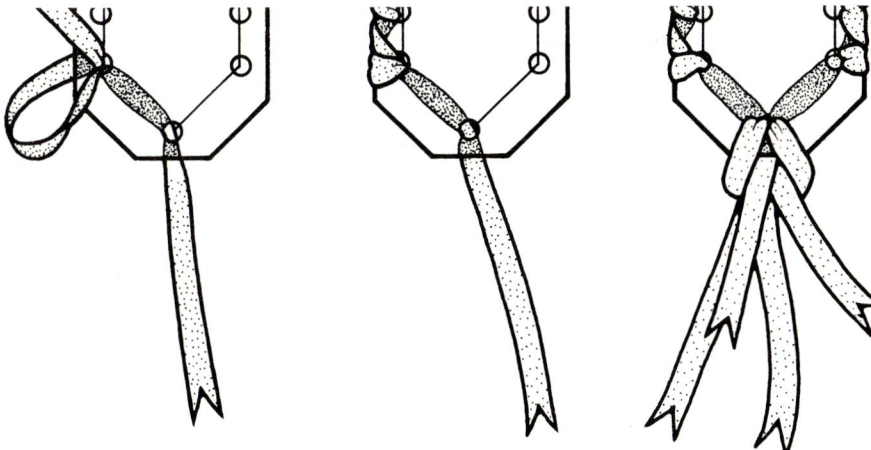

hole at the base, leaving 3″ trailing. (A large blunt needle can be used for this.) Pass the other end of the ribbon over the inner card and out of the first hole on the left side. Thread it twice through this hole by taking it over the left edge and up from below.

5 Continue drawing the ribbon evenly through each hole in turn as shown, taking it twice through the two top corner holes and twice through the last hole on the right side. Then take it between the folds of plastic and over the card, and down through the hole at the base. Cut the ribbon, leaving 3″ trailing.

6 Fold in half a $6\frac{1}{2}$″ length of the ribbon and thread the loop through the base hole from the back. Slip all four ribbon ends through this loop and draw up firmly.

Design 6

Materials
Thin coloured card $7\frac{1}{4}$″ by $1\frac{1}{2}$″
Hole-punch
1 yard ribbon $\frac{3}{8}$″ wide
$\frac{1}{4}$ yard braid 1″ wide
Clear adhesive

1 Cut a piece of thin coloured card $7\frac{1}{4}$″ long and $1\frac{1}{2}$″ wide. With a hole-punch make three holes at each end of the card and thirteen equi-distant holes down each side $\frac{1}{8}$″ from the edge.

2 From the back, draw 1 yard of ribbon through the hole at the base of the card, leaving 3″ trailing. Thread it neatly through all the punched holes, taking it twice through each corner hole. Finally pull the ribbon through the first hole and simply tie the two ends in a single knot.

3 Cut a piece of braid $7\frac{1}{4}$″ long and turn the ends under $\frac{1}{4}$″. With clear adhesive stick the braid down the centre of the card.

Hair ribbons

Especially suitable for parties, the hair decorations illustrated are made from short lengths of ribbon formed into bows and rosettes and stitched onto hair-slides (barettes) and hair-bands.

Bows A

Materials
18″ pink ribbon 2″ wide
Narrow slide (barette)

1. For a large double bow cut one 10″ piece and one 8″ piece of pink ribbon. Also cut a $1\frac{1}{8}″$ length to hold the bows at the centre.

2. Take the longer piece of ribbon and fold the two ends into the centre, allowing an overlap of $\frac{5}{8}″$. Make a row of running stitches down the centre of the overlap, draw up tightly, and fasten with two or three

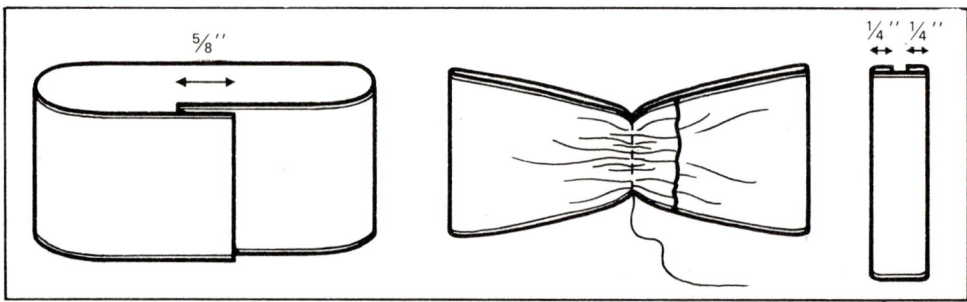

oversewing (overcasting) stitches. Repeat with the 8″ piece of ribbon and turn the raw ends of the centre piece of ribbon under $\frac{1}{4}″$.

3. Place the small bow on top of the large one, and hold the two together by encircling them with the centre piece. Stitch this in place at the back with an overlap of $\frac{1}{4}″$.

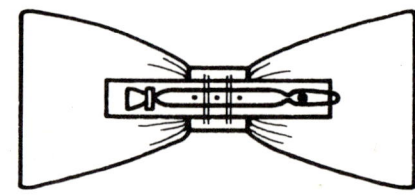

Bows: covering the slide with ribbon

4. Stitch a narrow slide or barette onto the back of the bows.

Bows B

Bows made following the above instructions can also be used with specially-shaped rubber bands (obtainable at large chain stores) for securing pony tails and plaits (braids). Make single bows about 2″ wide from 1″ wide ribbon and stitch them onto the rubber bands. For special occasions make three tiny bows from highly decorative ribbon (the kind used for Christmas parcels) and use velvet ribbon for the centre pieces. Cover a narrow slide or barette with a narrow piece of velvet ribbon,

turn the ends under, and oversew (overcast) the sides to hold the ribbon in place. Sew the three bows onto the velvet ribbon.

Hair ribbons

Rosette A

Materials
8" green ribbon 1" wide
10" pink ribbon $\frac{3}{8}$" wide
Small circular slide (barette)

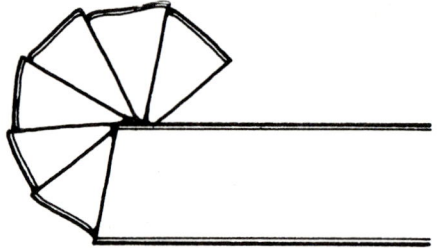

1 Rosette A

1. Cut an 8" piece of 1" or narrower green ribbon and make pleats along one edge to form a circle. Turn one raw end under and secure it with several tiny stitches to the top of the other raw end. Sew the pleats at the centre.

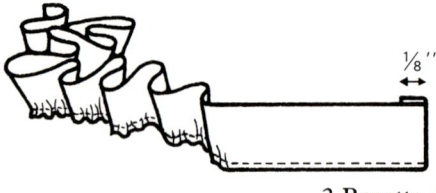

2 Rosette A

2. Take a 10" length of pink ribbon, turn one end under $\frac{1}{8}$", make a row of running stitches along one edge, and turn the other end under $\frac{1}{8}$". Gather up the running stitches tightly and fasten off, and the ribbon will of its own accord form a frilly flower-like rosette.

3. Sew the rosette into the centre of the pleated ribbon circle. If two different coloured ribbons are gathered together with the same row of running stitches, a pretty two-toned effect can be achieved.

4. Stitch the rosette onto a small circular slide or barette.

Rosette B

Materials
8" pink ribbon 2" wide
7" pink and gold ribbon $\frac{3}{4}$" wide
Small circular slide (barette)

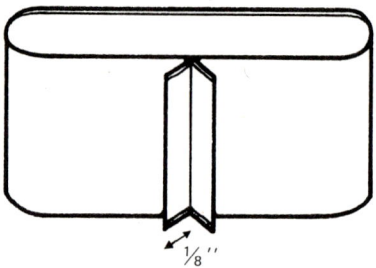

1 Rosette B

1. Cut an 8" piece of pink ribbon. Fold it in half and sew across the ends with tiny running stitches, allowing a $\frac{1}{8}$" seam. Turn the ribbon so that the seam is on the inside.

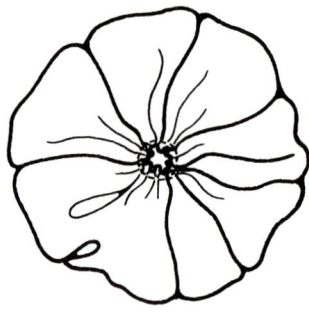

2 Rosette B

2. Make a row of running stitches along both edges. Gather up tightly and fasten off. Flatten the rosette into a circle and sew the gathered centres together.

3. For the central rosette cut a piece of pink and gold ribbon about 7" long. Turn the raw ends under $\frac{1}{8}$" and make a row of running stitches along the ribbon about $\frac{1}{4}$" in from one edge.

Hair ribbons

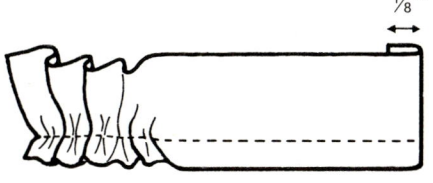

4 Rosette B

4 Draw the thread up tightly to make a small rosette. Make sure the gathered edges face outwards.

5 Sew the two rosettes together and finally stitch onto a small circular slide or barette.

Stars

Materials
$15\frac{1}{2}''$ red ribbon $\frac{1}{4}''$ wide
$10''$ pink and gold ribbon $\frac{3}{4}''$ wide
Circular slide (barette)

1 Cut a $15\frac{1}{2}''$ piece of $\frac{1}{4}''$ wide red ribbon (it must be $\frac{1}{2}''$ wide or less, otherwise the stars become too large). Make a loop of about $1''$ as shown, turning the ribbon over at the point of the star and returning it to the centre. Secure the ribbon at the centre with two or three stitches.

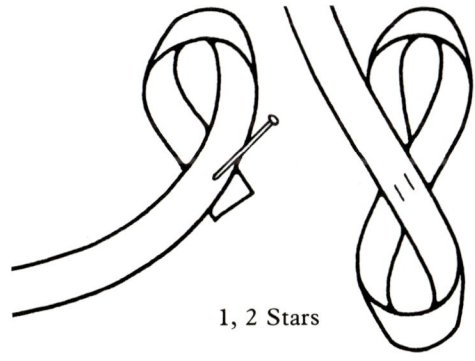

1, 2 Stars

2 Then make another loop, the same size as the first but in the opposite direction. Return the ribbon to the centre, securing it as before with several stitches. Continue in this way until six points are made to complete the star.

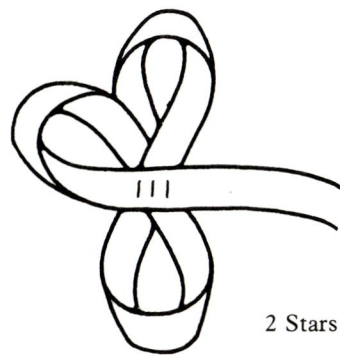

2 Stars

3 Cut off any excess ribbon but leave $\frac{1}{2}''$. Fold this under and sew it down at the centre.

3 Stars

4 Gather a $10''$ piece of pink and gold ribbon along one edge to make a rosette, and stitch this at the centre of the star. Alternatively, make a smaller star to stitch inside the larger one before adding a final rosette at the centre.

5 Stitch the star and rosette onto a circular slide or barette.

Roses

Hairbands

Materials
Piece of floral ribbon ¾″ wide (about 10″ long)
Piece of elastic (about 9½″ long)
Ribbon for bows and rosettes

Cut a piece of ¾″ wide floral ribbon to the length required (this will vary according to the age of the child). Fold the ends under ¼″ and stitch about a 9½″ length of elastic to the back of each end. Stitch bows or rosettes (made as described above) over the joining points of the ribbon and elastic.

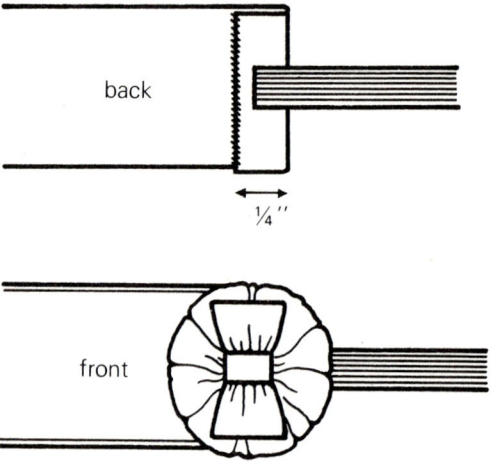

Roses

Ribbon roses can be made with stalks and used as a substitute for real flowers, or they can be made without stems and used for decorating hats or clothes. In each case the materials given are sufficient for making one stem, bud, bloom, or leaf.

Stem

Materials
9″ length of rustproof wire
10″ green ribbon ¼″ wide

To make the stems for the buds, full blooms, and leaf sprays, take a 9″ piece of wire and enclose it within a 10″ length of ribbon. Oversew (overcast) the ribbon along the length of the wire, neatening both ends by turning the ribbon back on itself before stitching down.

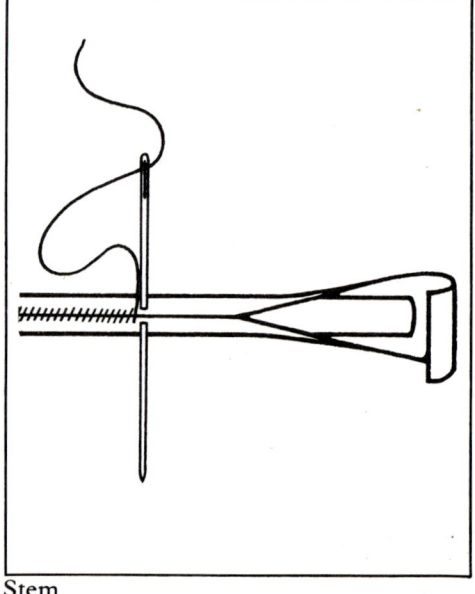
Stem

Roses

Bud

Materials
9" satin ribbon 2" wide (any colour)
Stem (as described above)
5" green ribbon ½" wide

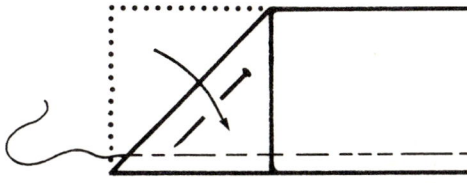

1 Bud

1 Take a piece of 2" wide satin ribbon 9" long, and with the wrong side uppermost, turn the ends over to make angles of 45°, and pin. Make a row of running stitches of unequal length along the bottom of the ribbon. Remove the pins, and gather the stitches.

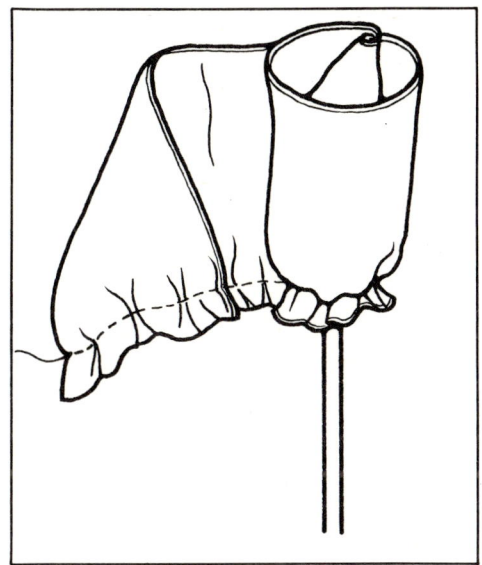

2 Bud

2 Encircle the top of the stem with the ribbon, using gathers and pleats to give the appearance of an opening bud. Stitch the base of the bud onto the ribbon of the stem.

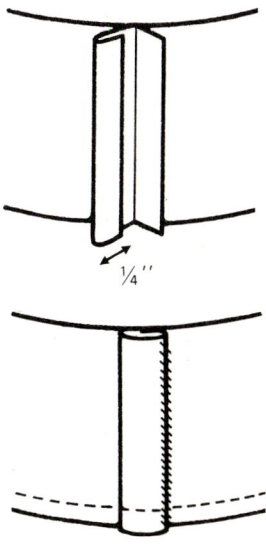

3 Bud

3 For the calyx fold a 5" piece of green ribbon in half and join the ends with a ½" seam to form a circle. Trim one end of the seam and fold the other end over it, turning the ribbon under ¼" so that all the raw ends are covered. Make a row of running stitches along one edge of the ribbon and gather up tightly to form a rosette, leaving a tiny hole at the centre for the stem.

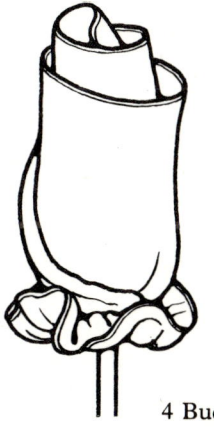

4 Bud

4 Slip the rosette onto the stem and stitch in place at the base of the bud.

Roses

Full bloom

Materials
Single bud (as described above)
1¼ yards satin ribbon 2″ wide

1 The opened roses are made from buds as described above (but note that the calyx is added at a later stage) with the addition of three or four ribbon petals. For each petal cut a piece of 2″ wide ribbon 6″ long at the top and 4″ long at the bottom. Cut the pieces alternately from either side of the length of ribbon to save wastage.

2 Make a row of running stitches along the two diagonals and the narrow edge of the ribbon, and gather. The ribbon will naturally assume a petal shape.

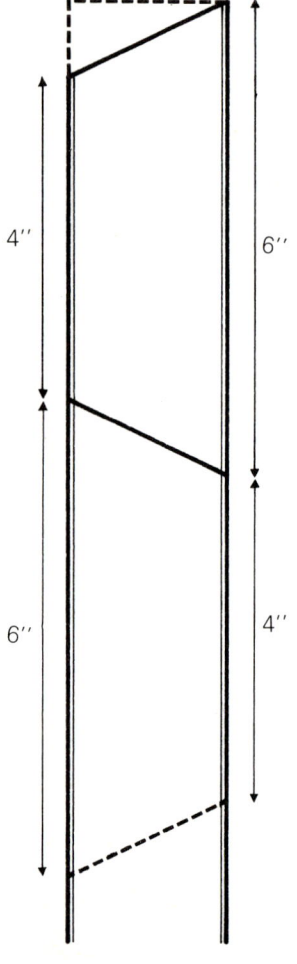

1 Full bloom

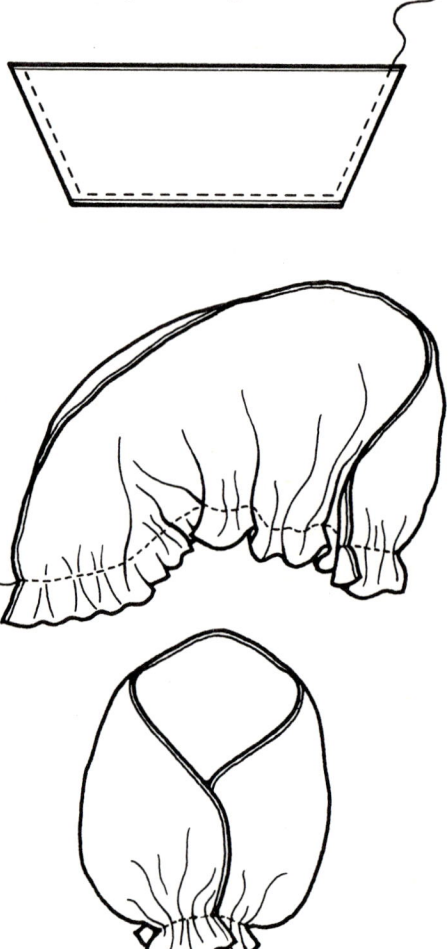

2 Full bloom

3 Overlap the edges at the base of the petal and secure with a few tiny stitches. Sew the petals onto the stem at the base of the bud.

4 Make a calyx of green ribbon as described above and stitch it in place at the base of the bloom. If any of the raw edges of the petals are visible, sew the calyx over them with a few random stitches.

Roses

Leaves

Materials
20" green ribbon $\frac{1}{2}$" wide
Stem (as described above)

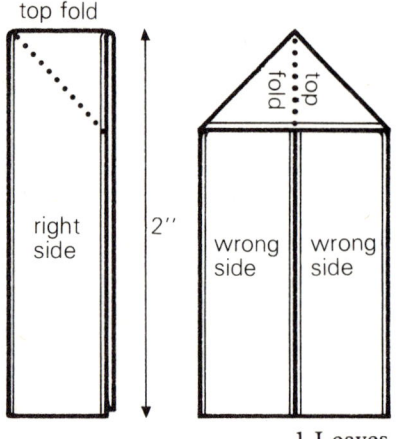

1 Leaves

1   Single leaves can be sewn onto the stems of buds and flowers or a complete leaf spray of five leaflets can be made on a separate stem. For each leaf cut a piece of green ribbon 4" long. Fold the ribbon in half, wrong sides together, then open out the side edges so that a point is formed at the top fold of the ribbon and the two halves are lying side by side.

2   Turn the two raw ends of ribbon diagonally outwards as shown and fold the ribbon in half so that all the folds and raw ends are enclosed.

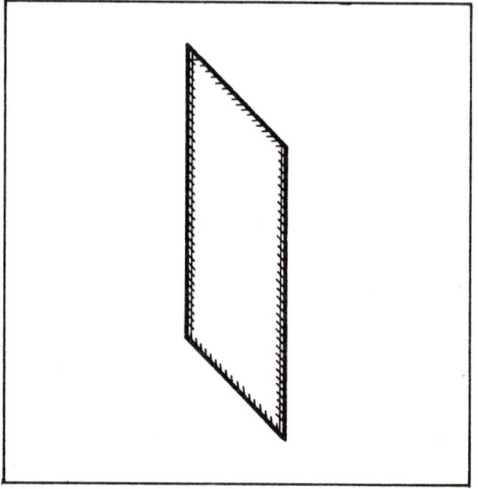

3 Leaves

3   Oversew (overcast) the edges of the ribbon and sew the leaf onto the covered stem at one corner.

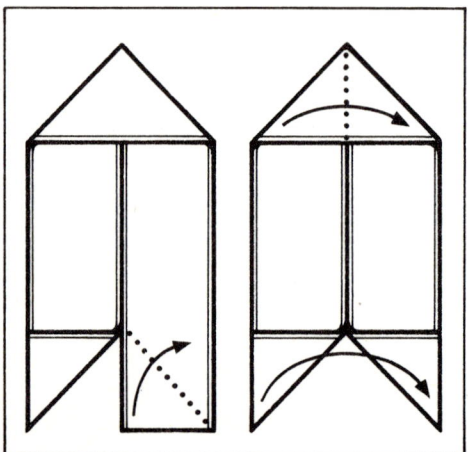

2 Leaves

Leaves: complete spray

Tank top

Ribbon must be knitted fairly loosely as unlike wool it has no elasticity, but even so, when knitted up, it produces an interesting springy texture. Many commercial patterns using very thick wool can be adapted for ribbon. The tank top illustrated is designed as an evening top but cotton tape could be used instead of ribbon to produce a more serviceable garment. The tension should be three stitches to the inch across, and three rows to the inch down.

Materials
Pair of no. 00 needles
52 yards dark blue ribbon ⅜" wide
66 yards mauve ribbon ⅜" wide
60 yards lilac ribbon ⅜" wide
No. 7 crochet hook

Using no. 00 needles and dark blue ribbon, cast on 43 stitches.

1st row Knit, work 17 rows in garter stitch.
19th row Change to mauve ribbon, knit, work 17 rows in garter stitch.
37th row Change to lilac ribbon and knit.
38th row Knit.
39th row Cast off 4 stitches, knit to last 4 stitches, cast off these last 4 stitches.
40th row Rejoin lilac ribbon, knit to end.
41st row Knit 1, knit 2 together, knit to last 3 stitches, knit 2 together, knit 1.
42nd row Knit.
43rd row Knit 1, knit 2 together, knit 6, cast off 15, knit 5, knit 2 together, knit 1.
44th row Knit across first set of stitches, join more lilac ribbon to other strap and knit, continue to knit both straps on same needle.
45th row Knit 1, knit 2 together, knit 2, knit 2 together, knit 1.
46th row Knit.
47th row Knit 1, knit 2 together (twice), knit 1.

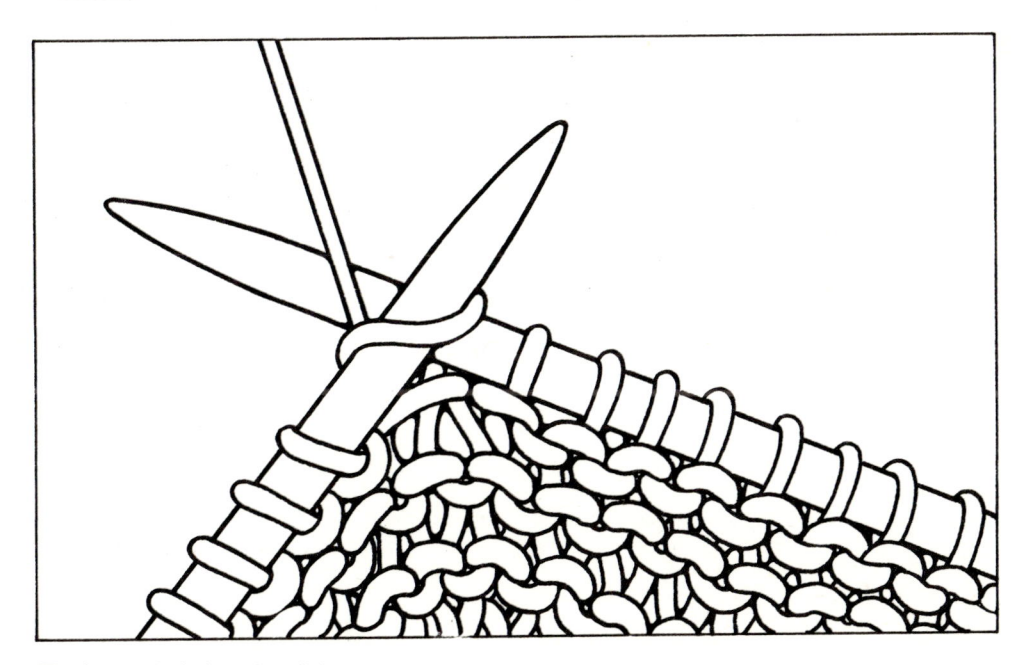

Tank top: knitting the ribbons

48th row Knit, knit 44 rows in garter stitch.
93rd row Knit 1, increase in next stitch, (twice), knit 1.
94th row Knit.
95th row Knit 1, increase in the next stitch, knit 2, increase in the next stitch, knit 1.
96th row Knit.
97th row Knit 1, increase in the next stitch, knit 4, increase in next stitch, knit 1, cast on 15 stitches, knit across 16 stitches, increase in next stitch, knit 4, increase in next stitch, knit 1.
98th row Knit.
99th row Knit 1, increase in the next stitch, knit to last 2 stitches, increase in next stitch, knit 1.
100th row Knit.
101st row Cast on 4 stitches, knit to end.
102nd row Cast on 4 stitches, knit to end.
103rd row Knit.

Fringes

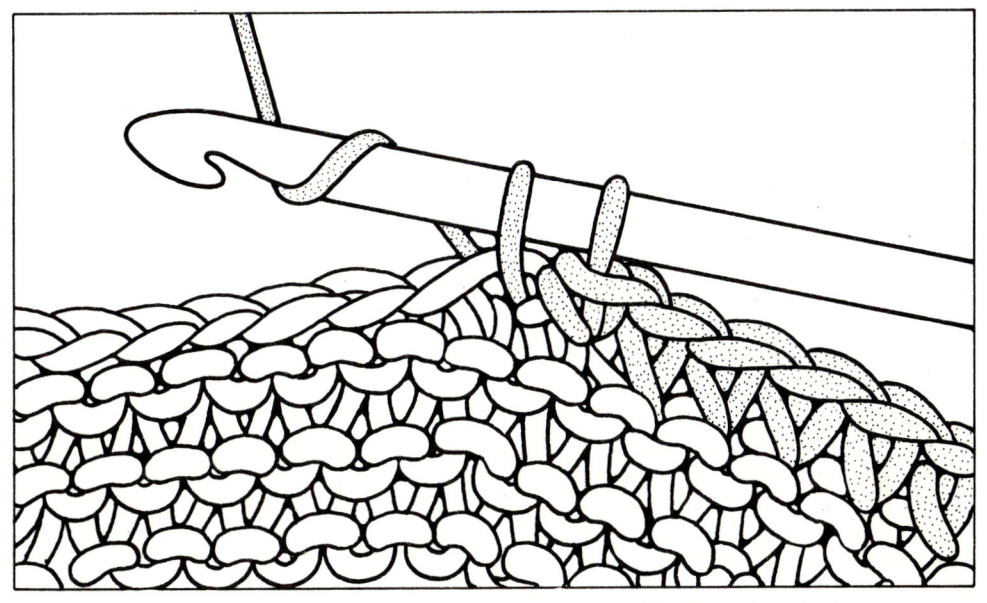

Tank top: crocheting the edges

Change to mauve ribbon and work 18 rows in garter stitch. Change to dark blue ribbon and work 18 rows in garter stitch. Cast off. Sew up the side seams.

Using lilac ribbon and no. 7 crochet hook, double crochet all round the arm holes, neck, and bottom of the garment.

Fringes

The fringes illustrated are intended to decorate roller blinds but they can be used successfully on cushions, clothes, tablemats, etc. Curved effects cannot be achieved as ribbons have no bias, but this can be compensated for by folding at angles to form zigzag lines, and many different designs can be made by varying the length and width of the ribbons and the spaces between them. The fringes are best made on ribbon bases (backing ribbon) which can then be sewn to the bottom of the blinds at the back. In each case the quantities given are for decorating one foot of blind.

Red fringe

Materials
13" red backing ribbon $\frac{3}{4}$" wide
$\frac{3}{4}$ yard red ribbon $\frac{1}{4}$" wide
1$\frac{3}{4}$ yards blue cord ribbon $\frac{1}{8}$" wide
7 white beads
$\frac{3}{4}$ yard braid $\frac{5}{8}$" wide

1 Take a red backing ribbon and, starting in the middle (to ensure both sides are equal), place marker pins at 1$\frac{1}{2}$" intervals on the wrong side.

37

Fringes

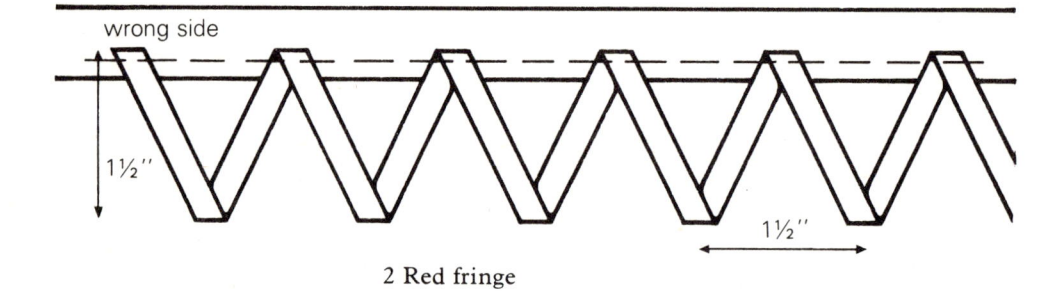

2 Red fringe

2 With ¼" wide red ribbon, make a fringe folded diagonally as shown at the 1½" intervals. Tack along the edge of the backing ribbon so that the fringe is held in place at the top of every V. Make sure the depth of the Vs remains constant at 1½".

3 Measure and cut seven 4" lengths of blue cord ribbon. Thread a white bead onto each, fold them in half, and tack in place at the top of every red ribbon V.

3 Red fringe

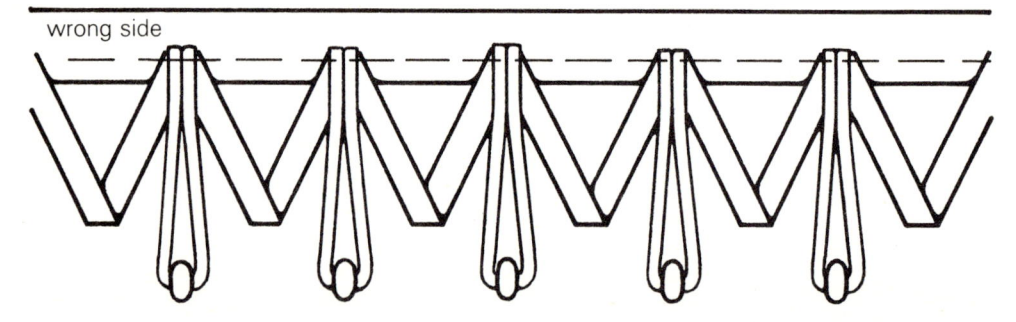

4 Pin and tack the backing ribbon plus fringe to the base of the blind at the back, such that the fringe is held between the blind and the backing ribbon, and turn the ends under ½". Sew in place and remove all three sets of tacking.

5 Pin and tack two lengths of braid along the bottom of the blind, one at the base and the other 1" above the base, turning the ends under ½". Stitch along both edges.

Blue fringe

Materials
2 yards blue ribbon ¼" wide
Curtain ring
13" blue backing ribbon ¾" wide
¾ yard of wide blue ric-rac braid

1 Cut sixteen 2½" pieces of ¼" wide blue ribbon and one 6½" piece for the centre ribbon.

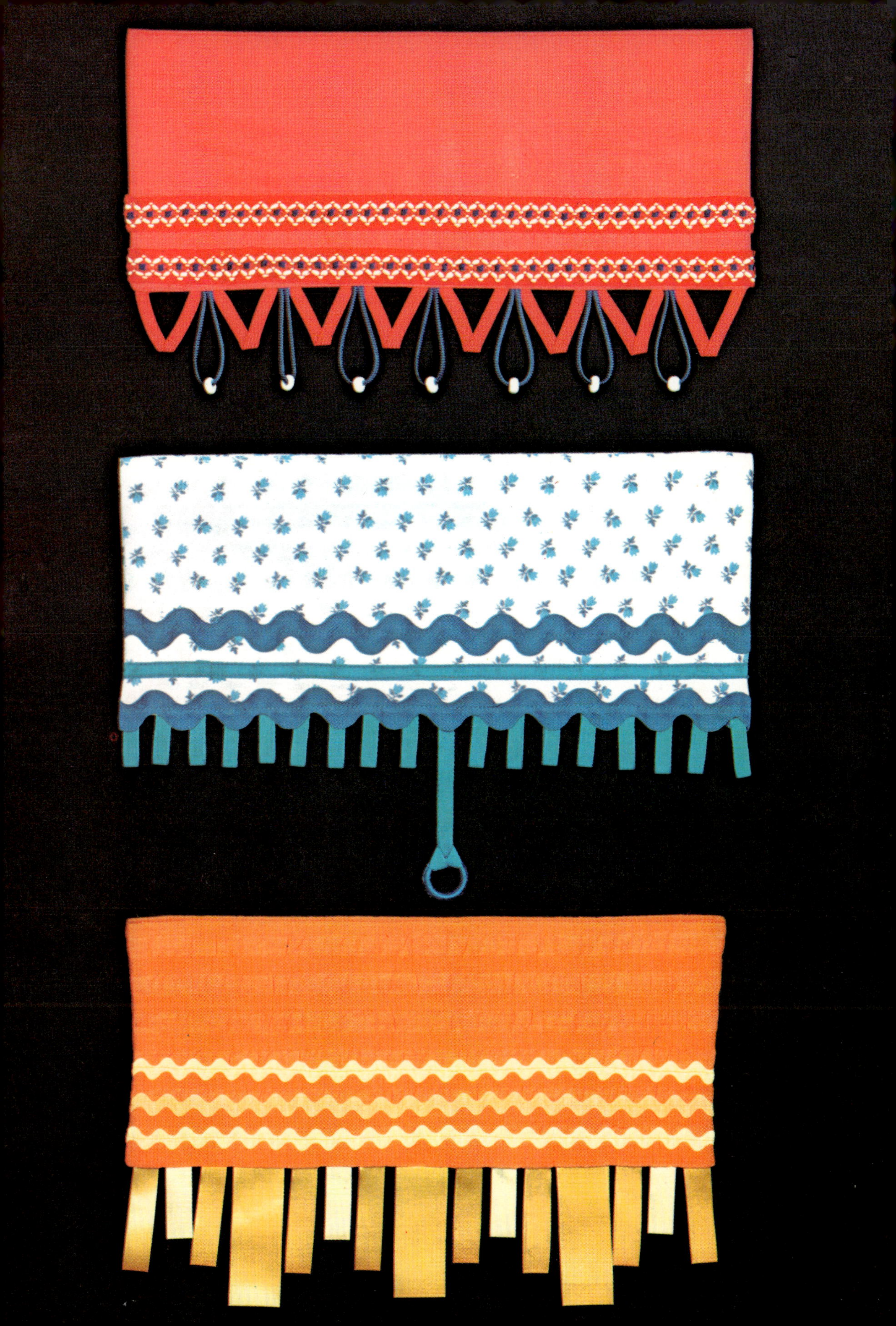

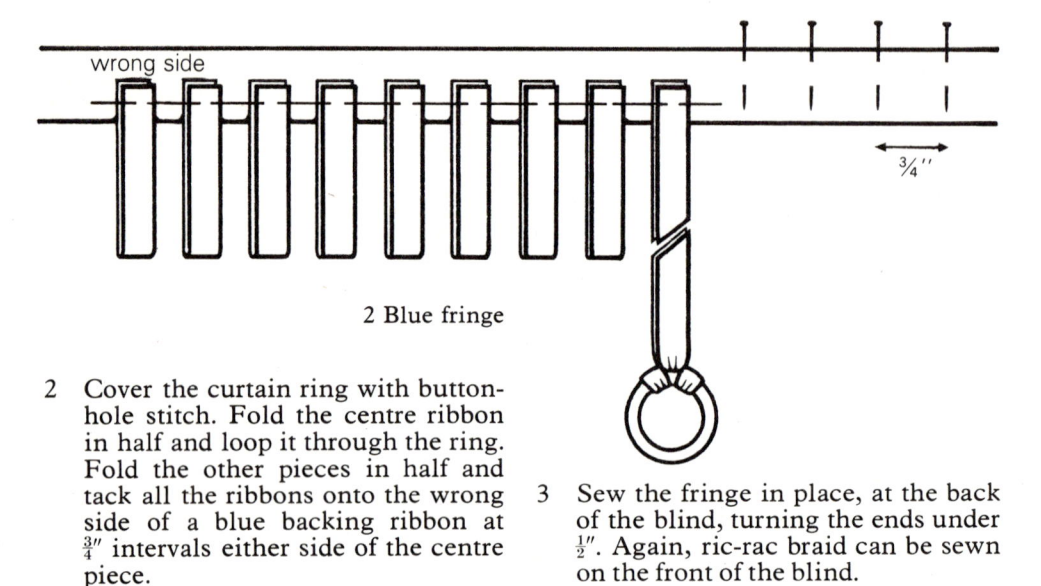

Fringes

2 Blue fringe

2 Cover the curtain ring with buttonhole stitch. Fold the centre ribbon in half and loop it through the ring. Fold the other pieces in half and tack all the ribbons onto the wrong side of a blue backing ribbon at $\frac{3}{4}''$ intervals either side of the centre piece.

3 Sew the fringe in place, at the back of the blind, turning the ends under $\frac{1}{2}''$. Again, ric-rac braid can be sewn on the front of the blind.

Yellow fringe

Materials
$\frac{1}{2}$ yard golden yellow ribbon 1" wide
$1\frac{1}{4}$ yards golden yellow ribbon $\frac{1}{2}''$ wide
$\frac{1}{2}$ yard lemon yellow ribbon $\frac{1}{2}''$ wide
13" orange backing ribbon $\frac{3}{4}''$ wide
$1\frac{1}{4}$ yards of narrow yellow ric-rac braid

1 Cut three 6" lengths of 1" wide golden yellow ribbon, eight 5" lengths of $\frac{1}{2}''$ wide golden yellow ribbon and four 4" lengths of $\frac{1}{2}''$ wide lemon yellow ribbon, and fold each piece in half.

2 Pin one of the pieces of folded 1" wide golden yellow ribbon to the centre of an orange backing ribbon. Next to this pin a folded $\frac{1}{2}''$ wide golden yellow ribbon, a folded $\frac{1}{2}''$ wide lemon yellow ribbon, and then another folded $\frac{1}{2}''$ wide golden yellow ribbon. Continue this process on either side of the central ribbon to form a scalloped edge, leaving spaces in-between of $\frac{3}{16}''$.

3 Tack all the fringe ribbons in place and then stitch the backing ribbon to the back of the blind, turning the ends under $\frac{1}{2}''$. Ric-rac braid can be sewn onto the bottom front of the blind if desired.

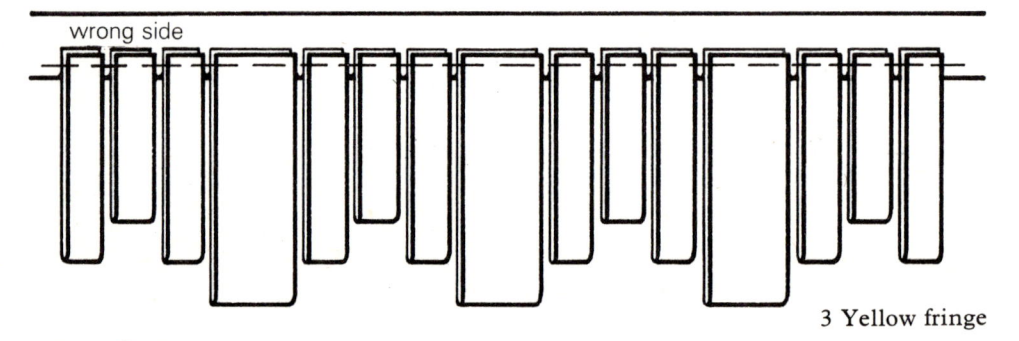

3 Yellow fringe

Fringes

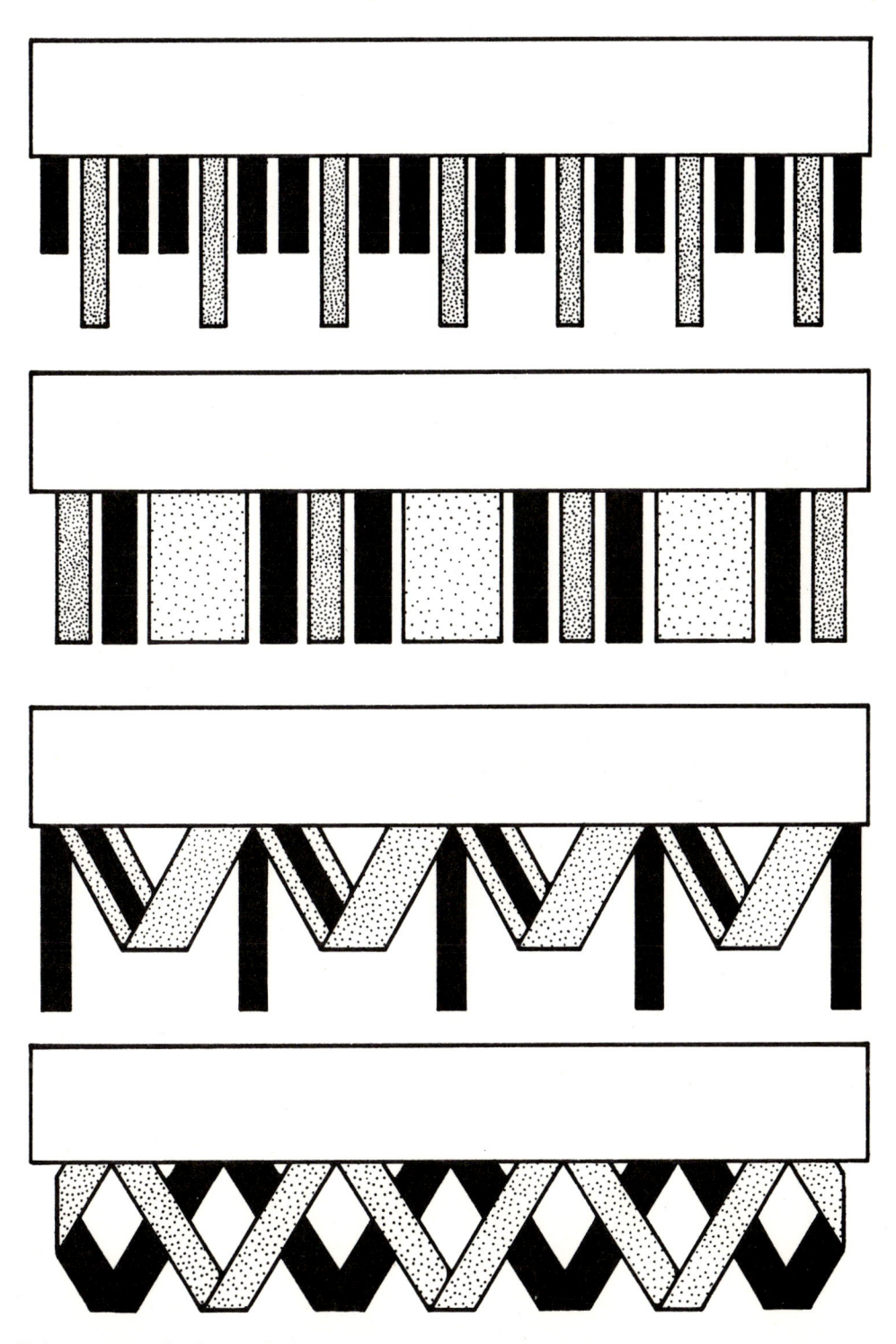

Fringes: some further variations

41

Velvet cushion cover

It is relatively easy to greatly enhance the look of any cushion by the addition of velvet ribbon. The cover illustrated is made with the ribbon sewn in a linear pattern.

Materials
$\frac{1}{2}$ yard strong cotton 36″ wide for cushion cover
$1\frac{3}{4}$ yard lengths of velvet ribbon $1\frac{3}{8}$″ wide in cream, brown, black, and ochre
$16\frac{1}{2}$″ square filled cushion.

1 Cut the strong cotton into a rectangle $34\frac{1}{2}$″ by 18″. Mark the centre point on the left-hand side of the cushion — this will be 9″ down from the top and 9″ in from the left edge (allowing for a $\frac{3}{4}$″ seam all round).

2 Cut each of the four pieces of velvet ribbon into the following lengths: $2\frac{3}{8}$″, $5\frac{1}{8}$″, $7\frac{7}{8}$″, $10\frac{5}{8}$″, $13\frac{3}{8}$″, and $16\frac{1}{8}$″.

Velvet cushion cover

1 Velvet cushion cover

3 Velvet cushion cover

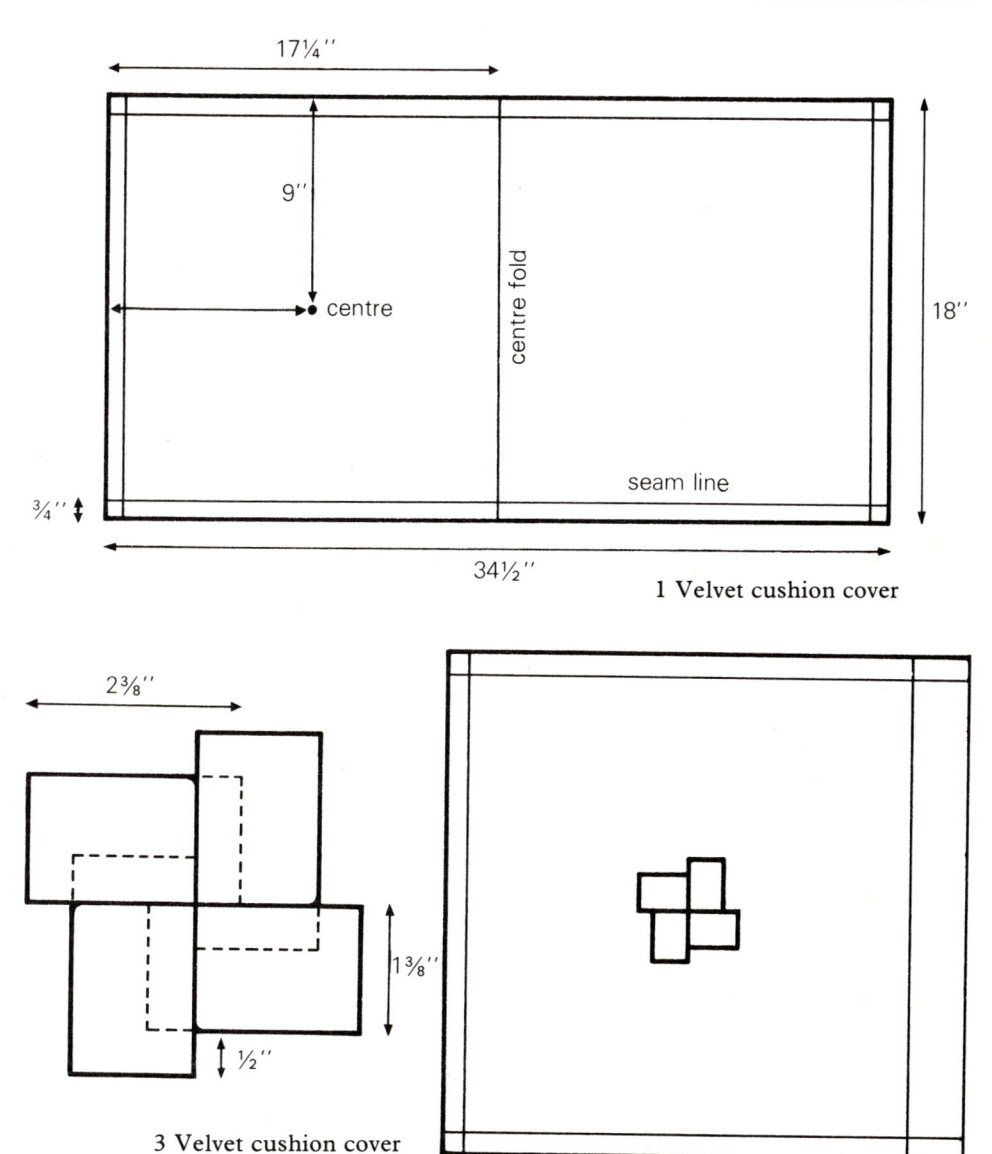

3 Take the four shortest lengths of ribbon (2⅜″) and pin them at the centre of the cushion cover to form the beginnings of a square shape. They should be positioned at right angles to each other, in such a way that one raw end of each is covered by the side edge of another. At this stage the ribbons in fact make a windmill shape as the other raw ends extend for ½″ beyond the square, but these ends will be covered by the next round of ribbons. Check that the velvet pile runs towards the centre of the cushion.

43

Velvet cushion cover

4   Tack and then sew the ribbons in place by hand with tiny running stitches down both sides of each one. It is advisable not to use machine stitching as the ribbons tend to gather up and will not lie flat.

5   Add the next round of four ribbons, keeping the same sequence of colours and overlapping the raw ends of the previous round. Again check the direction of the pile. Sew the ribbons in place.

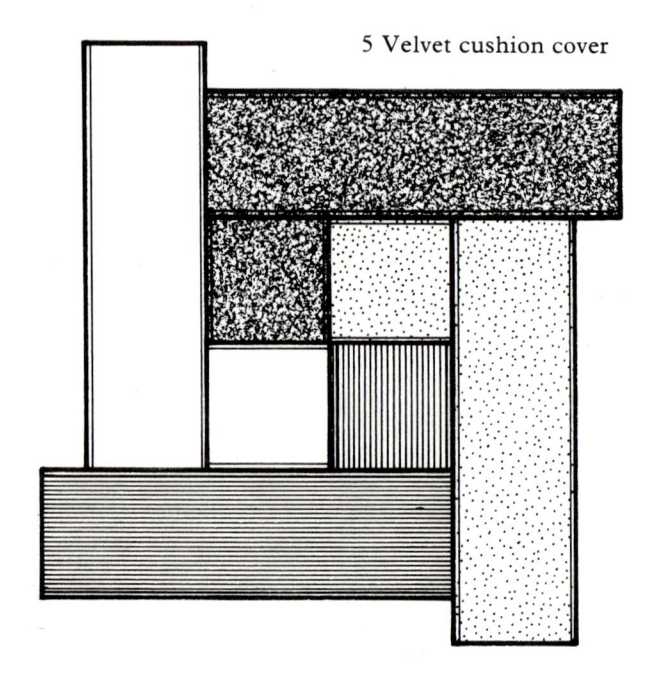

5 Velvet cushion cover

6   Continue adding rounds of ribbon, stitching each in place before adding the next. At the four corners of the final round turn the raw ends under $\frac{1}{2}''$ and stitch down.

7   Fold the cover in half, right sides together, and sew up the two sides, allowing a $\frac{3}{4}''$ seam. Oversew (overcast) these edges on the inside.

8   Turn the cover the right way out and slide it over the filled cushion. Turn under the two remaining raw edges and oversew (overcast) them to enclose the cushion.

Peg dolls

Many different types of dress can be adapted for the dolls (those illustrated are dressed as traditional peasants), although the proportions may have to be altered and simplification of design will be necessary.

Materials
Wooden clothes-pegs (pins) about 4" long
Sandpaper
Paint (acrylic or enamel)
Indian ink
Pipe cleaners
Embroidery silk (or cotton) for hair
Clear adhesive
Odd remnants of ribbon in various widths and textures

The doll
1 Sandpaper any rough areas on the peg especially around the 'face' and on the 'legs'.

2 Paint the legs of the peg with enamel paint to represent the doll's stockings, and the tips of the peg as shoes. Paint or draw in the face of the doll. It is best to use Indian ink as this is permanent and does not smudge. Felt tip pens could be used but the colour tends to spread into the wood.

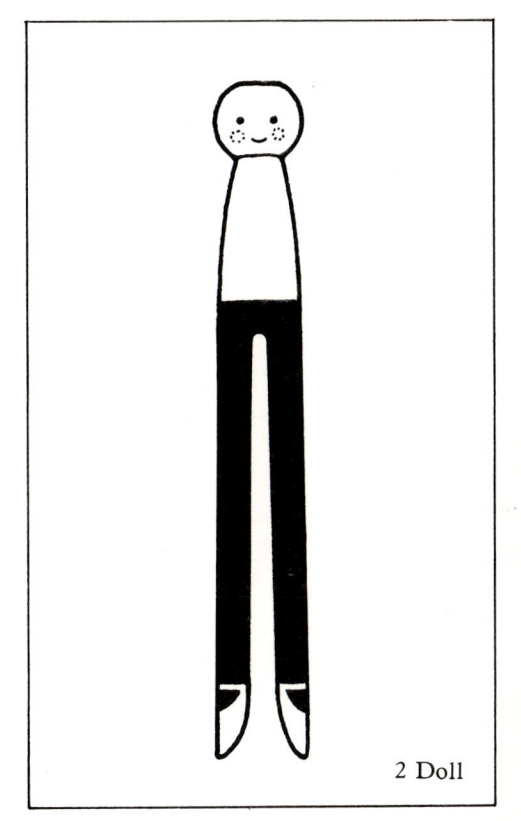

2 Doll

3 Cut a 4½" length of pipe cleaner for the arms and fold each end back ¼" to form the hands.

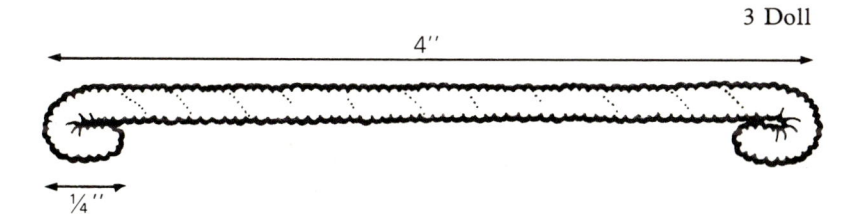

3 Doll

4 Measure out strands of embroidery silk about 5" long for the hair. Stitch the strands together across the centre and stick onto the peg with clear adhesive. The hair can be plaited, left loose, tied back in bunches, or made into a tiny bun.

Peg dolls

Dressing the doll

1 The blouse sleeves are made from a 4″ piece of 1″ wide ribbon. Turn the ends under ¼″ and fold lengthwise over the pipe cleaner. Oversew (overcast) along the edges and gather and secure at the wrists.

1 Dressing the doll

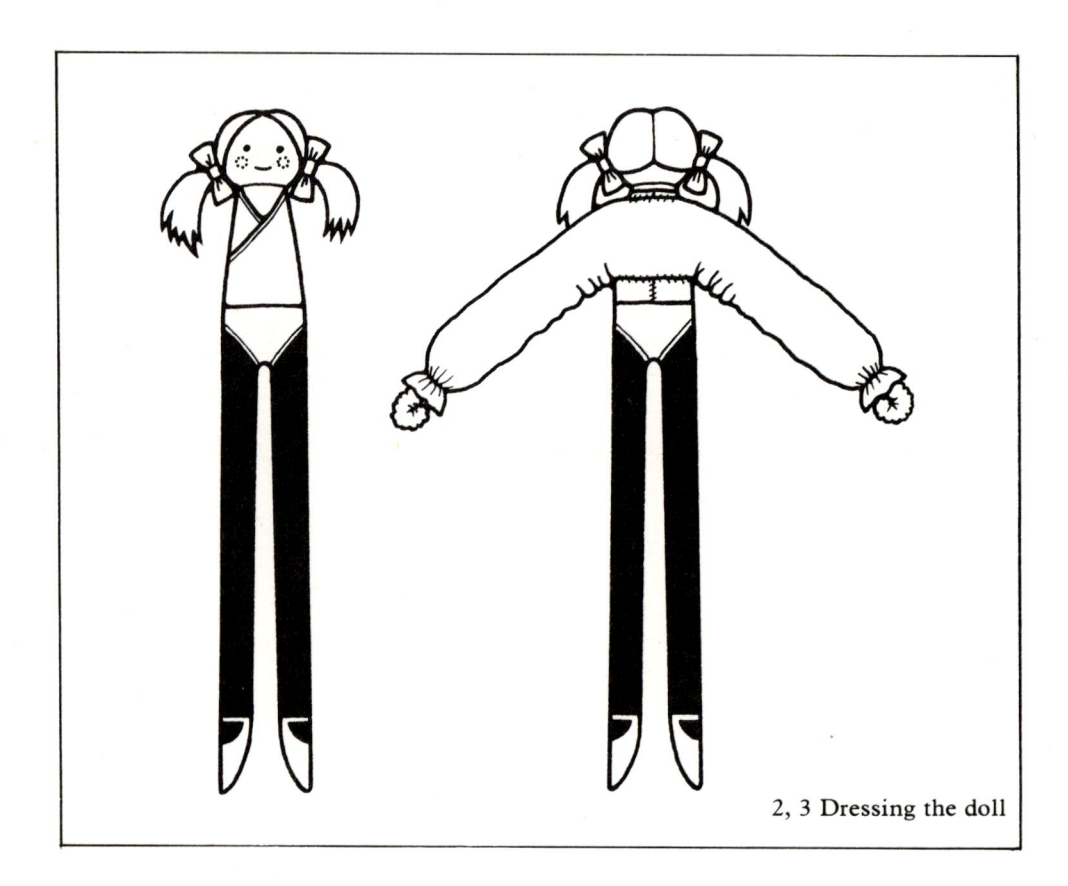

2, 3 Dressing the doll

2 Slip a small piece of 1″ wide ribbon between the doll's legs and stitch at each side of the body to form the pants.

3 To make the bodice wrap a length of ribbon the same colour as the sleeves around the peg and secure at the back. Stitch the arms to the bodice across the back and the shoulders.

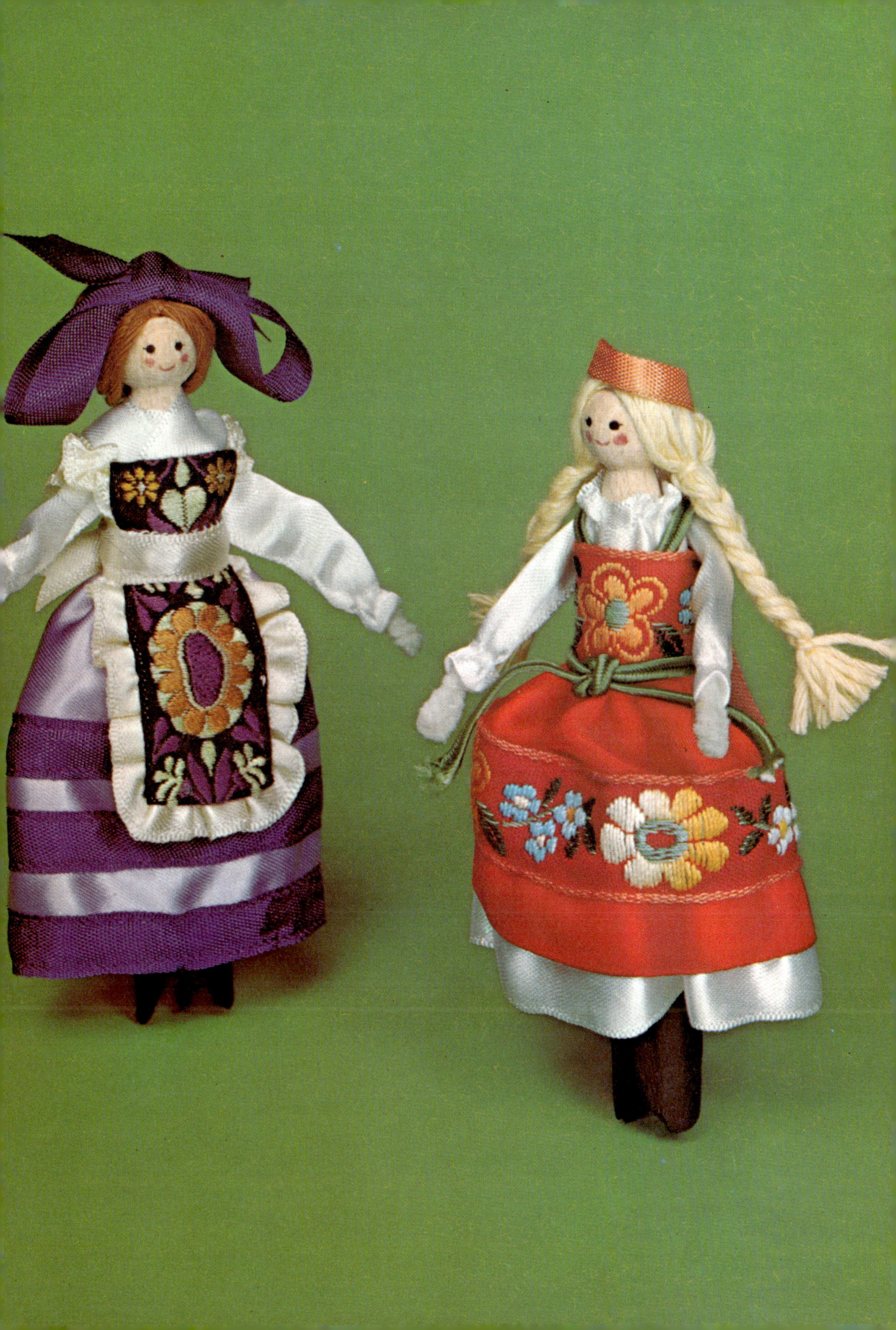

Peg dolls

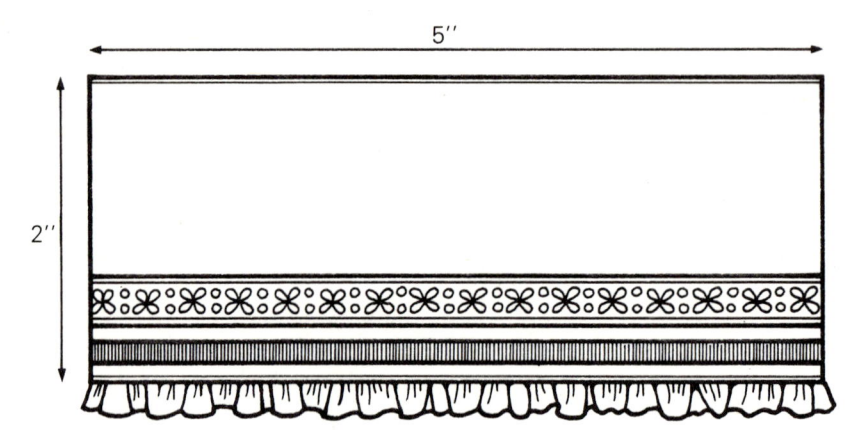

4 Dressing the doll

4 Cut a piece of 2" wide ribbon 5" or 6" long for the skirt and decorate it by machining narrow ribbons or braid onto it or by adding a frill of contrasting ribbon at the bottom. With right sides together, machine up the side seam. Turn the skirt the right way out and gather at the top with small running stitches. Stitch the skirt onto the bodice at the waist.

5 For the head-dress, either simply stitch a bow onto the hair, or stitch in place a tiny band tied at the back.

6 Additional decorations such as pinafores, belts, boleros, etc. can easily be made from small pieces of narrow ribbon or braid.

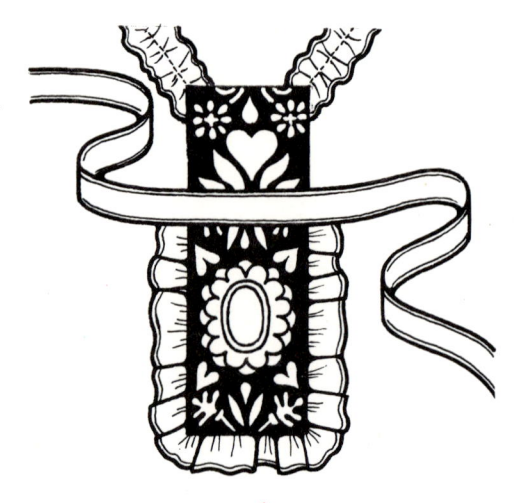

6 Dressing the doll

48

Belts

Belts can be made to look very attractive, especially if colours that match clothes are chosen. They can be fastened in several ways, including buckles (with or without prongs), snap fasteners, or hooks and eyes, all depending on the desired effect. Large waist measurements will require slightly more ribbon than is allowed for here.

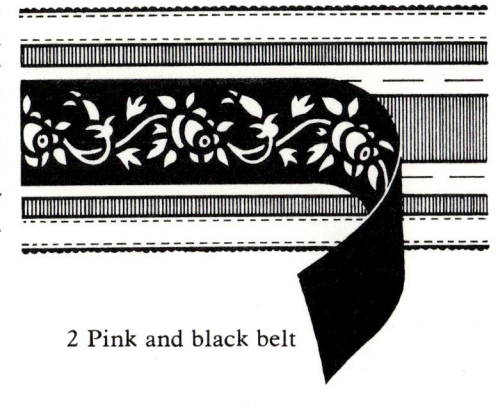

2 Pink and black belt

Pink and black belt

Materials
1 yard black petersham or grosgrain ribbon 2" wide
2 yards pink ribbon $\frac{1}{4}$" wide
2 yards lime ribbon $\frac{1}{4}$" wide
1 yard fancy braid or ribbon $\frac{3}{4}$" to $\frac{7}{8}$" wide
Buckle
Hole-punch or riveting kit

1 Cut a piece of black petersham (grosgrain) ribbon the same length as the required waist measurement plus 5". Sew two lengths of pink ribbon along each edge of the petersham using two rows of stitching.

2 Tack two rows of lime ribbon $\frac{1}{8}$" in from the pink rows, but do not sew them. Tack the braid down the centre of the belt, partially overlapping the two lime rows. Sew down either edge of the braid – this will also hold the lime ribbon in place. Remove all tacking stitches.

3 With right sides together, fold one end of the belt in half lengthwise and stitch firmly across the ends, allowing a $\frac{1}{4}$" seam. Trim off the corner, fold right side out, and press down to form the pointed end of the belt.

3 Pink and black belt

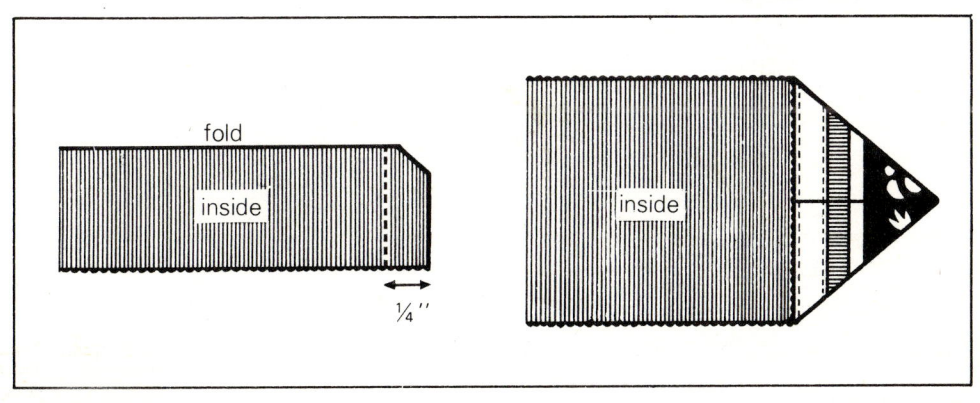

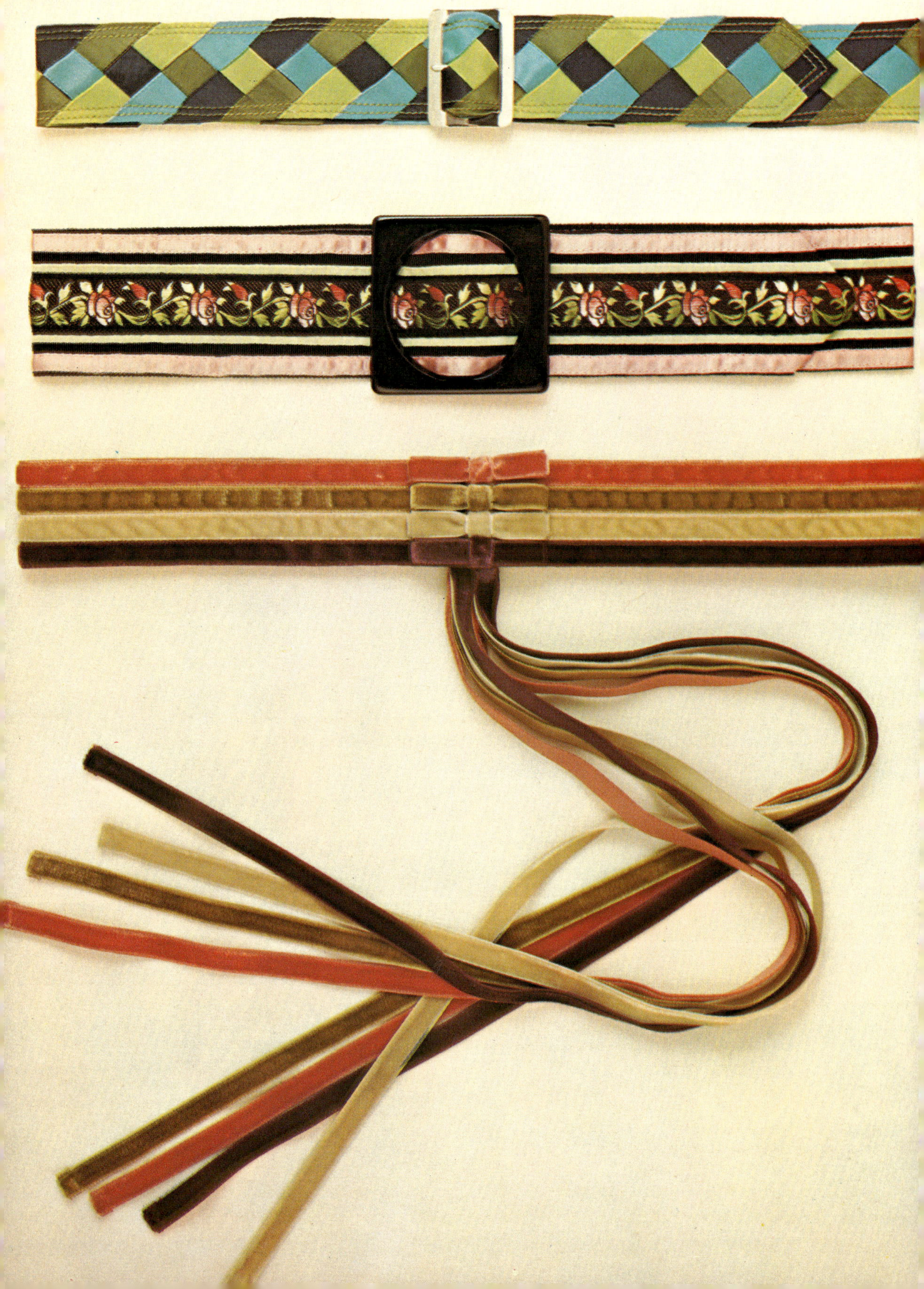

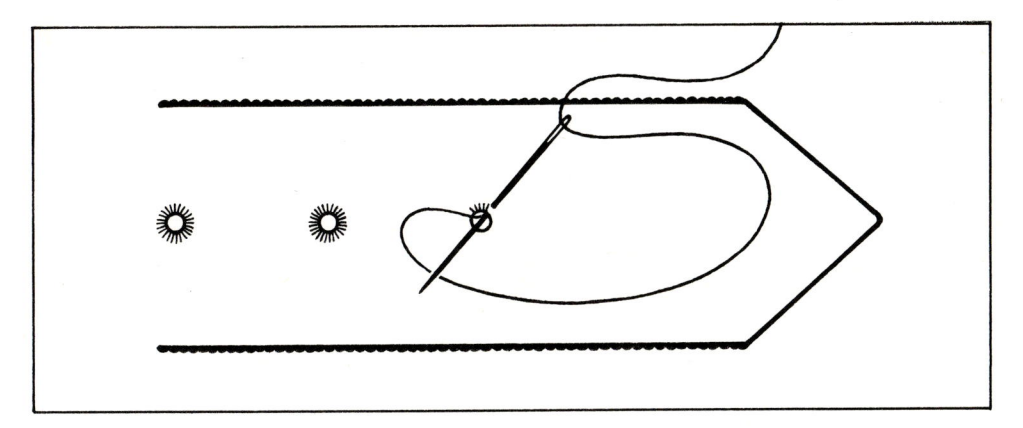

Belts

4 Pink and black belt

4 Choose a suitable buckle and stitch into place by turning the end of the belt over the central bar. If the buckle has a prong, use a hole-punch to make three or four holes at the pointed end 1" apart. Neaten each hole with buttonhole stitch or alternatively use a riveting kit.

Striped velvet belt

Materials
1 yard petersham or grosgrain ribbon 1½" wide
4 pieces of velvet ribbon ⅜" wide and 1½ yards long in pink, olive, cream, and purple
2 snap fasteners (snappers or poppers)

1 Cut a piece of petersham (grosgrain) ribbon the length of the waist measurement plus 2⅜", and four lengths of velvet ribbon in four different colours the length of the waist measurement plus 1".

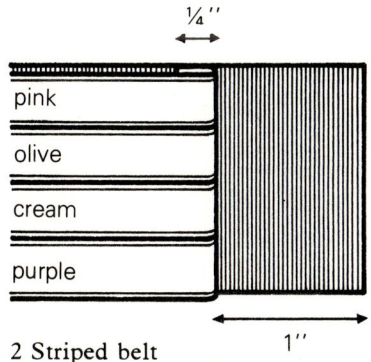

2 Turn one end of each velvet ribbon under ¼" and pin them side by side on top of the petersham 1" from the end, in the order pink, olive, cream, purple. At the other end the petersham will extend ⅝" beyond the raw ends of the velvet ribbons. Tack and then sew the velvet ribbons in place. Remove tacking stitches.

3 Cut two 18" lengths of ribbon of each colour for the strands that trail from the middle of the belt. Turn the hanging ends of each under ⅛" twice, and stitch.

4 Place the ribbons on top of each other in two groups of four, in the same order as the belt and with purple on top. Stitch each group together, and then sew them to the back of the belt at the end where the petersham extends for 1" beyond the velvet ribbons.

2 Striped belt

51

Belts

5 Fold the petersham back over the raw ends of the trailing ribbons, allowing a ¼″ turn, and stitch down. At the other end of the belt fold the ⅝″ of petersham over onto the right side to cover the raw ends of the lengthwise velvet ribbons, again allowing a ¼″ turn, and stitch down.

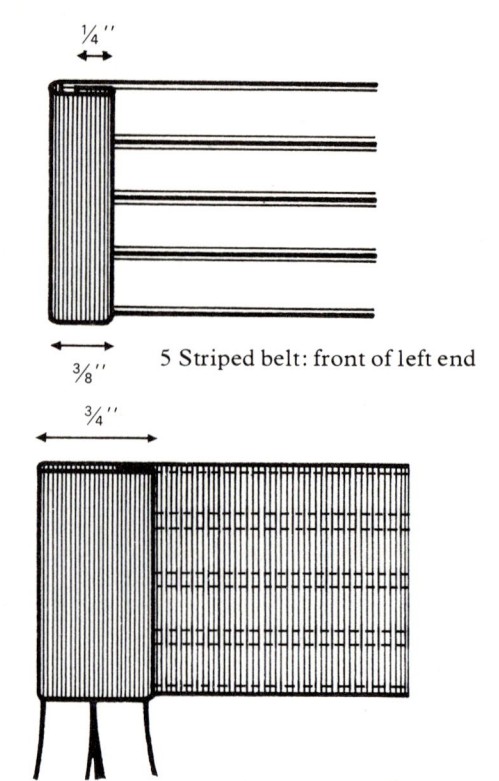

5 Striped belt: front of left end

5 Striped belt: back of right end

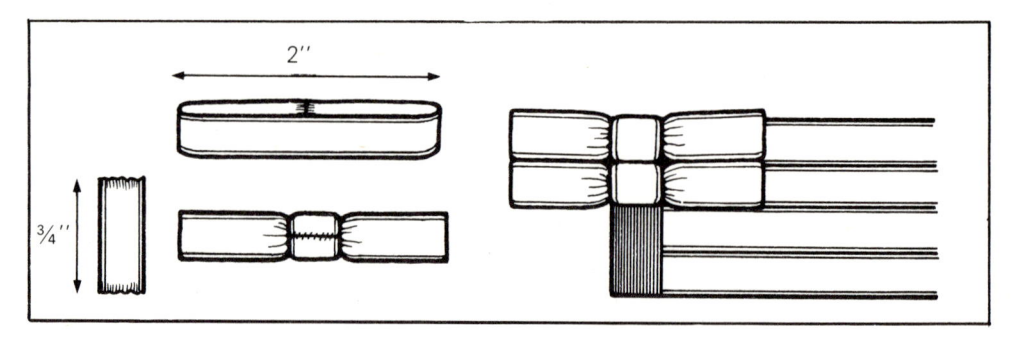

6 Striped belt

6 Make four little bows with 4″ lengths of velvet ribbon, folding each length in half with the ends at the centre. Cover the joins with ¾″ lengths of ribbon and stitch these in place at the back of the bow. Sew the bows onto the petersham at the opposite end to the trailing ribbons.

7 Sew on two sets of snap fasteners (snappers or poppers) such that when the belt is worn, the trailing ribbons are positioned behind the bows.

Abstract Picture

Plaited belt

Materials
4 pieces of ribbon $\frac{1}{2}''$ wide and $1\frac{3}{4}$ yards long in navy, olive, blue, and lime
1 yard petersham or grosgrain ribbon $1\frac{1}{4}''$ wide
Buckle
Hole-punch

1   For a belt to fit a 24" to 26" waist, take $1\frac{3}{4}$ yards of ribbon in navy, olive, blue, and lime (for larger sizes increase the length to 2 yards), and plait (braid) the ribbons as shown, tacking along the edges as the plait grows to hold it in place. It may be found easier if the ends are pinned down before starting.

2   Following the pattern of the plait, make one end pointed by folding the ribbon ends under. Then tack the plait onto a backing petersham (grosgrain) ribbon and finish with two rows of stitching all round the edge.

3   Stitch the buckle in place and, if necessary, make holes for the prong as before.

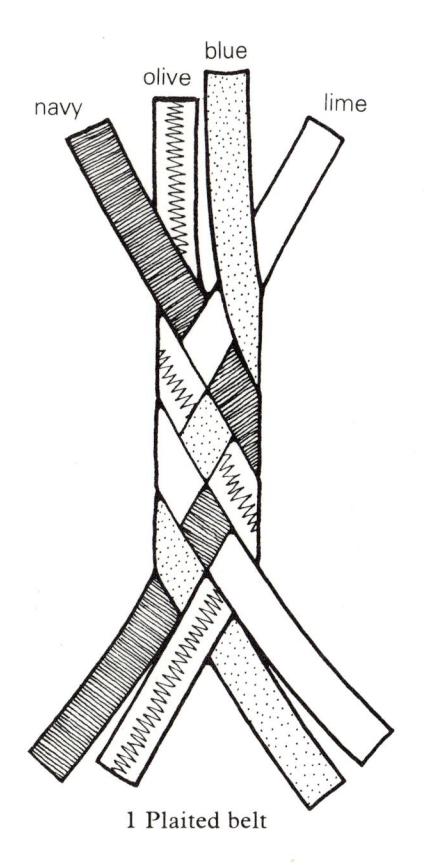

1 Plaited belt

Abstract picture

The most important factor when making a picture with ribbons is finding a suitable design. If inspiration is elusive, search through old magazines and reference books. Look again at familiar objects such as the patterns made by books on shelves, a framework of iron girders, or the folds in a piece of material. Consider natural objects, the grain in wood, leaf patterns, rock strata—the source of ideas is endless.

Materials
Paper for the colour rough
Ribbons and braids in various widths and textures
Backing material: plain cotton or rayon, or any closely-woven material
Cardboard the same size as the finished picture
Two plastic curtain rings

1   Once a design has been decided on, select a colour system and calculate approximately how much ribbon will be needed. Remember that all the pieces have to be machined down onto the background material so limit the number of colours to two or three shades, otherwise continuous changing of the machine thread will be necessary.

Abstract picture

2 Make a colour rough of the design to work from. This need not be the same size as the finished picture but it must be in proportion. The picture illustrated is 21" by 24".

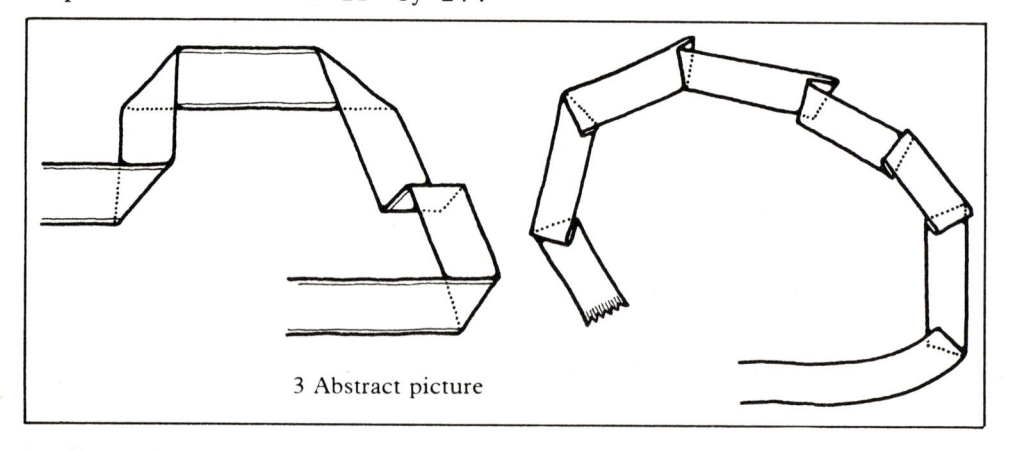

3 Abstract picture

3 Cut a piece of backing material the size of the finished picture plus a border of 2" all round. On the right side pin the pieces of ribbon that form the basis of the design. They need not lie in straight lines but can be folded to form curves and circular shapes. Some people may find it a help if the backing material is held taut (by pins or a frame) while arranging the ribbons.

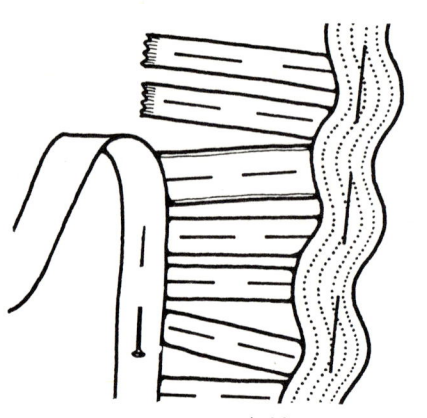

4 Abstract picture

4 When the main framework of the design is pinned in position, continue building up the picture by adding smaller lengths of ribbon. All raw ends should be neatened either by turning them under or by covering them with a length of another ribbon.

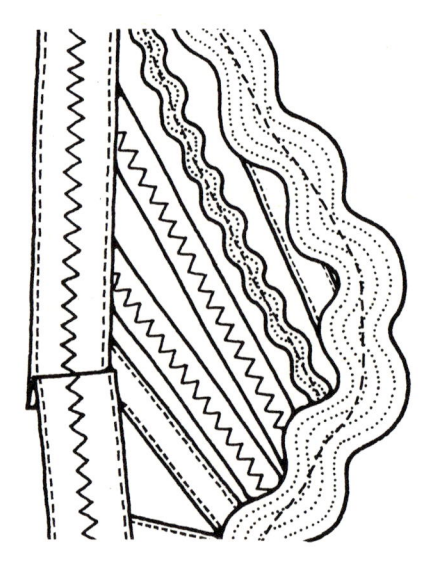

5 Abstract picture

5 Tack the ribbons carefully into place on the background material so that the picture is ready for machine stitching. This can either take the

54

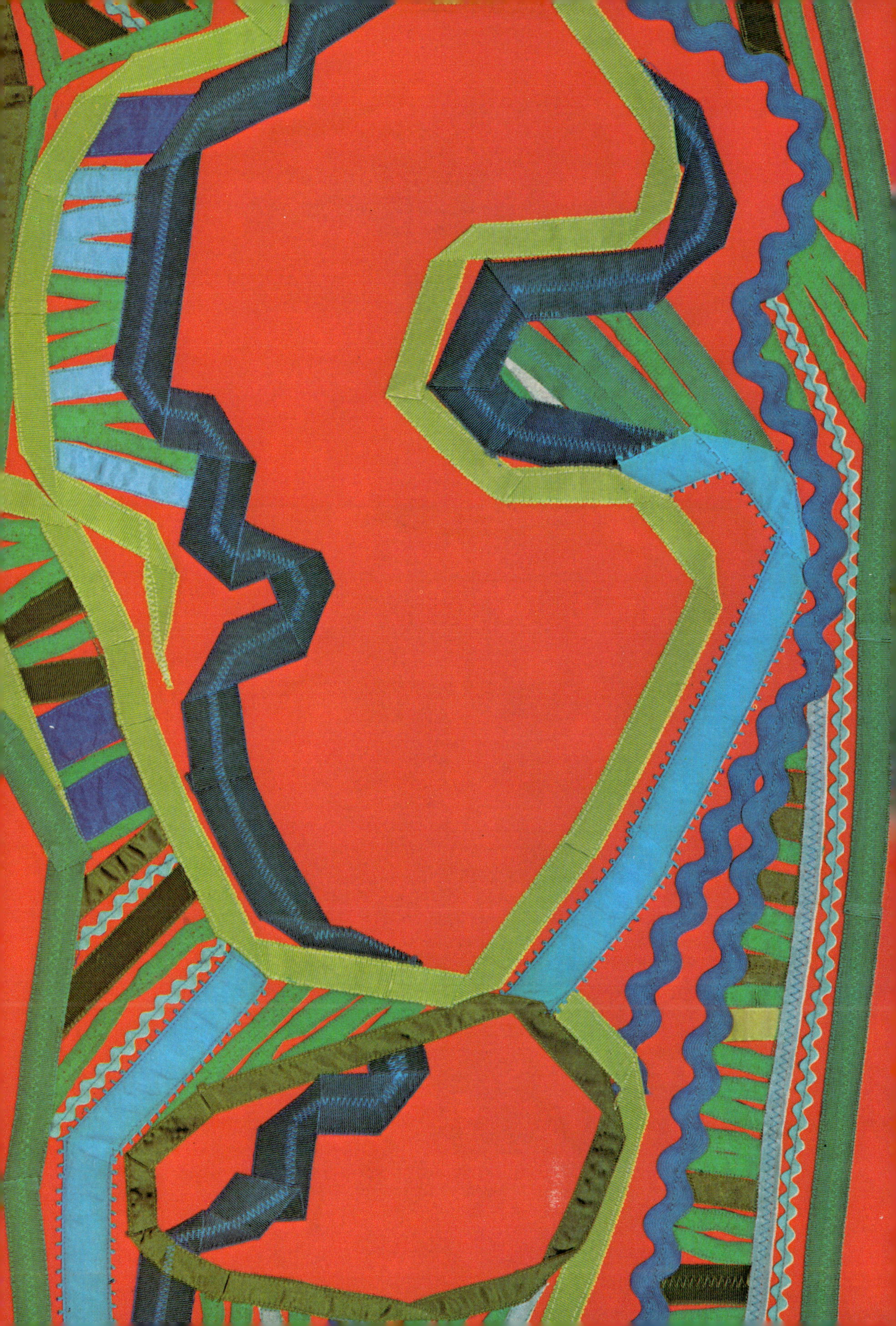

Abstract picture

form of securing stitches or it can be part of the pattern by making a line of zigzag stitches in a contrasting colour along the length of some of them. For ribbons narrower than $\frac{1}{2}''$, a single line of stitching is sufficient, but those wider than $\frac{1}{2}''$ should be held in place by a line of stitching along either edge.

6 Remove all tacking and press the finished picture.

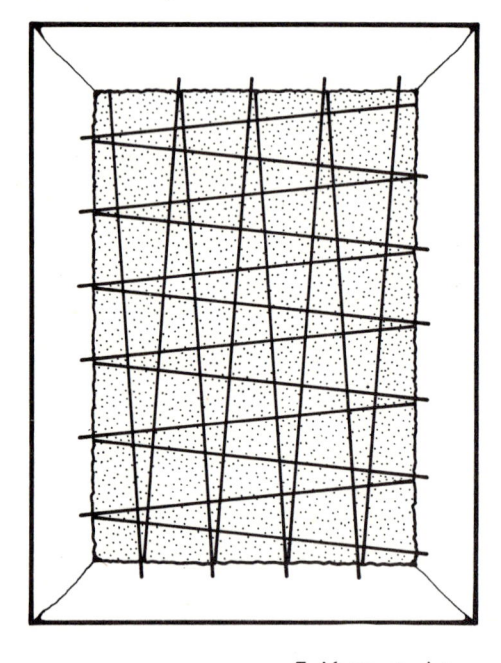

7 Abstract picture

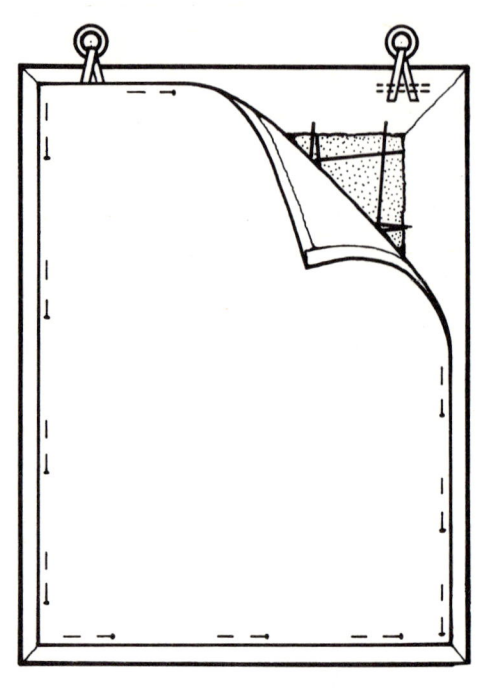

9 Abstract picture

9 Cut another piece of backing material, this time the same size as the finished picture and turn the edges under $\frac{1}{2}''$. Pin this onto the back of the picture covering the ribbons of the hangers, and stitch into position.

7 Place a piece of firm cardboard onto the back of the picture. Turn over the 2" border, fold in the corners, and secure with large zigzag stitches.

8 Take two small plastic curtain rings (metal ones can be used but they tend to tarnish) and thread a piece of ribbon 2" long and $\frac{1}{2}''$ wide through each. Place these at the top left and right-hand corners at the back of the picture, about 2" in from each edge, and stitch the ribbons securely in place.

Aprons

Although aprons are functional there is no reason why they should not be made more attractive by the addition of ribbon. As well as being decorative in the form of frills and strips, the ribbon can also be practical for neck and waistbands. The measurements given for the waisted apron and the pinafore make medium-sized garments.

Waisted apron

Materials
1 yard pink denim 36" wide
Piece of tracing or brown paper about 12" square
3 yards white ribbon $\frac{1}{2}$" wide
$3\frac{1}{4}$ yards red ribbon $\frac{1}{4}$" wide
$3\frac{1}{2}$ yards orange ribbon $\frac{1}{4}$" wide
4 yards yellow ribbon $\frac{1}{2}$" wide
4 yards green ribbon $\frac{1}{4}$" wide
4 yards turquoise ribbon $\frac{1}{4}$" wide
4 yards blue ribbon $\frac{1}{2}$" wide
$3\frac{3}{4}$ yards purple ribbon $\frac{1}{4}$" wide

1. Cut a rectangle of pink denim 36" by $24\frac{1}{2}$" for the skirt of the apron and two strips 36" long and $4\frac{1}{2}$" wide for the waistband.

2. On a piece of paper draw an irregular star shape with an internal diameter of approximately 6". Use either tracing paper or brown wrapping paper, but not newsprint as the ink can mark the material. Cut out the shape and pin it in the middle of the pink denim rectangle, slightly nearer the top to allow for a $1\frac{1}{2}$" hem at the bottom.

3. Pin white ribbon onto the material following the outside edge of the paper shape. Fold the ribbon over at the points of the star.

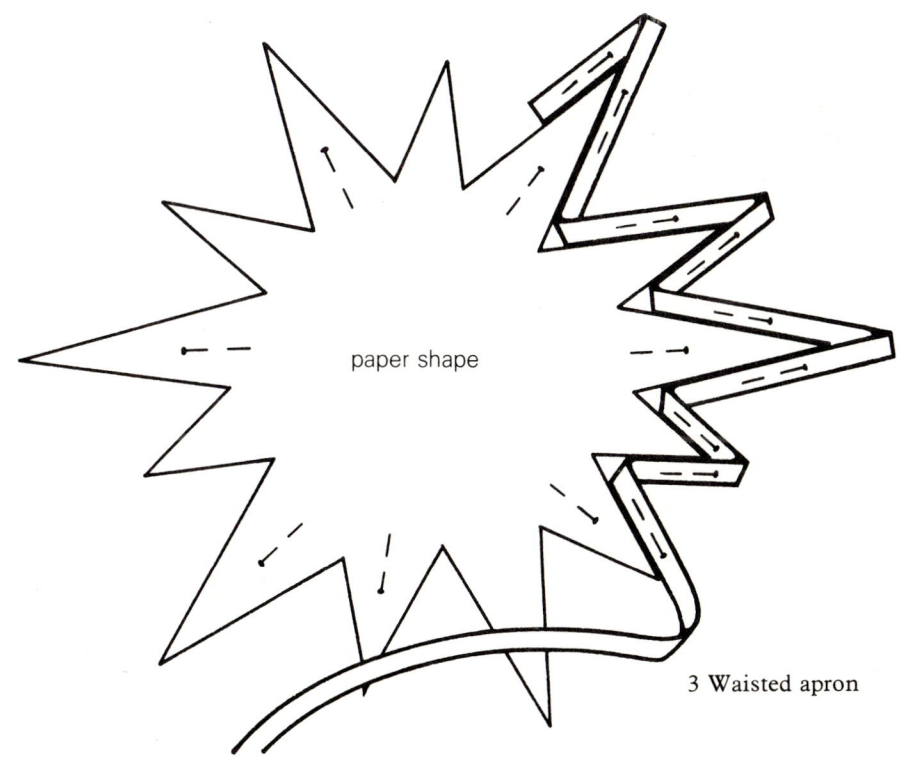

3 Waisted apron

Aprons

4 Where the two ends meet, join them by folding one end under ½" and pinning it over the other end. This is best done about half-way along one of the edges of the star points. Remove the paper shape, tack the white ribbon in place, and then stitch along both edges.

5 Following the same star shape, pin the red ribbon onto the denim about 1" out from the white ribbon and tack and stitch in place. Similarly sew the other six lengths of ribbon onto the apron in the order orange, yellow, green, turquoise, blue, and purple, but leave a space of approximately ½" between each one. It will be found that only part of the outer stars will fit onto the apron. When the stitching is complete, remove all tacking and press.

6 Sew ½" hems down each side of the skirt. If the sides are selvedge edges just turn under once but if the edges are raw turn under ¼" twice. Make a 1½" hem round the bottom of the apron.

7 With a pin, mark the centre point of the waist of the skirt. On either side and 1⅝" away from this point make and pin several outward-facing pleats, adjusting the number according to the required waist size. These should be about ½" deep and at intervals of 1". Secure the pleats with a double row of tacking stitches.

8 For the waistband join the two 4½" wide strips of pink denim together with a ½" seam to form a longer strip. Fold the band in half along its length with right sides facing, and make a ½" seam across either end. Trim away the corners.

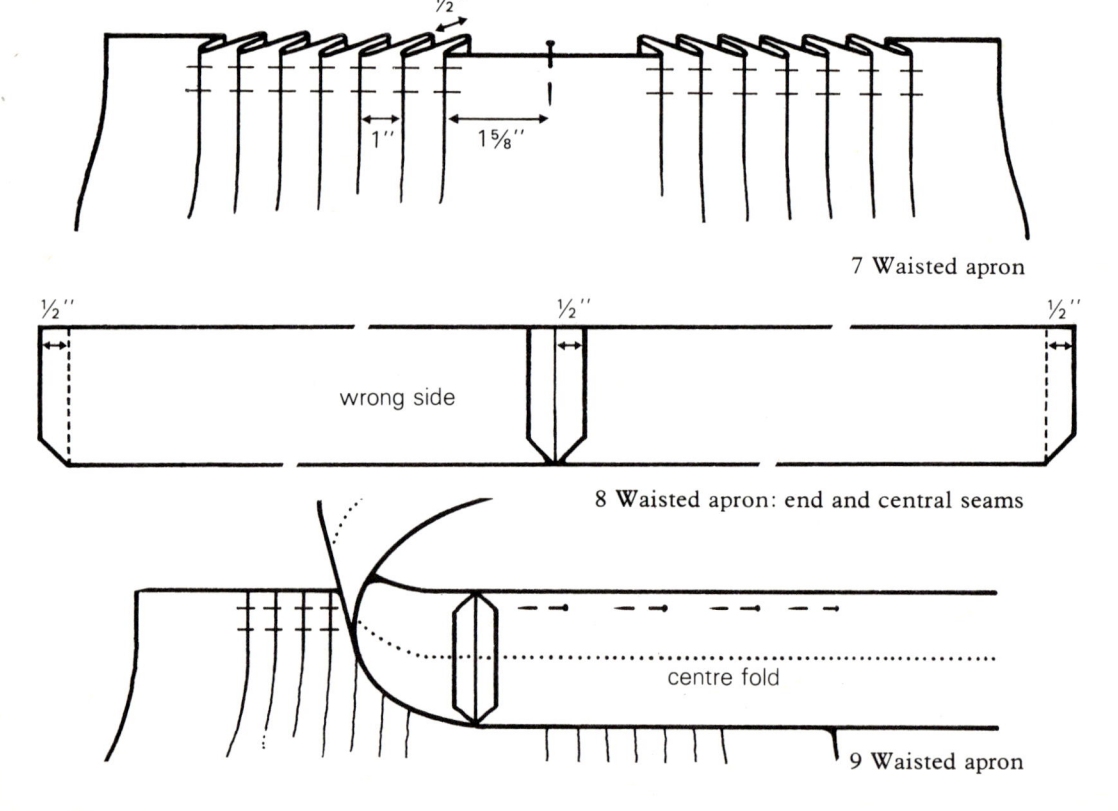

7 Waisted apron

8 Waisted apron: end and central seams

9 Waisted apron

Aprons

9 Turn the waistband the other way out and pin it with right sides facing along the top edge of the apron skirt, matching the central seam of the waistband with the marker pin at the centre of the skirt. Tack in place and stitch firmly making a seam $\frac{1}{2}''$ from the top edge. Remove all tacking.

10 Turn all the remaining raw edges of the waistband under $\frac{1}{2}''$ and pin in place. Turn the waistband over so that the right side is uppermost, fold over again, and pin onto the skirt at the back, enclosing all the turned edges. Tack and stitch along the complete length of the top and bottom edges and the ends of the waistband and then remove all tacking.

Child's apron

Materials
$\frac{3}{4}$ yard blue sail-cloth 36" wide
$\frac{1}{4}$ yard yellow sail-cloth 36" wide
$1\frac{1}{4}$ yards lime ribbon $\frac{1}{2}''$ wide
$1\frac{1}{2}$ yards pale blue ribbon 1" wide
$2\frac{1}{4}$ yards yellow ribbon $1\frac{1}{2}''$ wide
2 snap fasteners (snappers or poppers)

1 For the two main parts of the apron cut a large rectangle 21" by $22\frac{1}{2}''$ and a small rectangle $10\frac{1}{4}''$ by 12" out of blue sail-cloth, such that one $10\frac{1}{4}''$ side of the small rectangle and one 21" side of the large rectangle are selvedge edges.

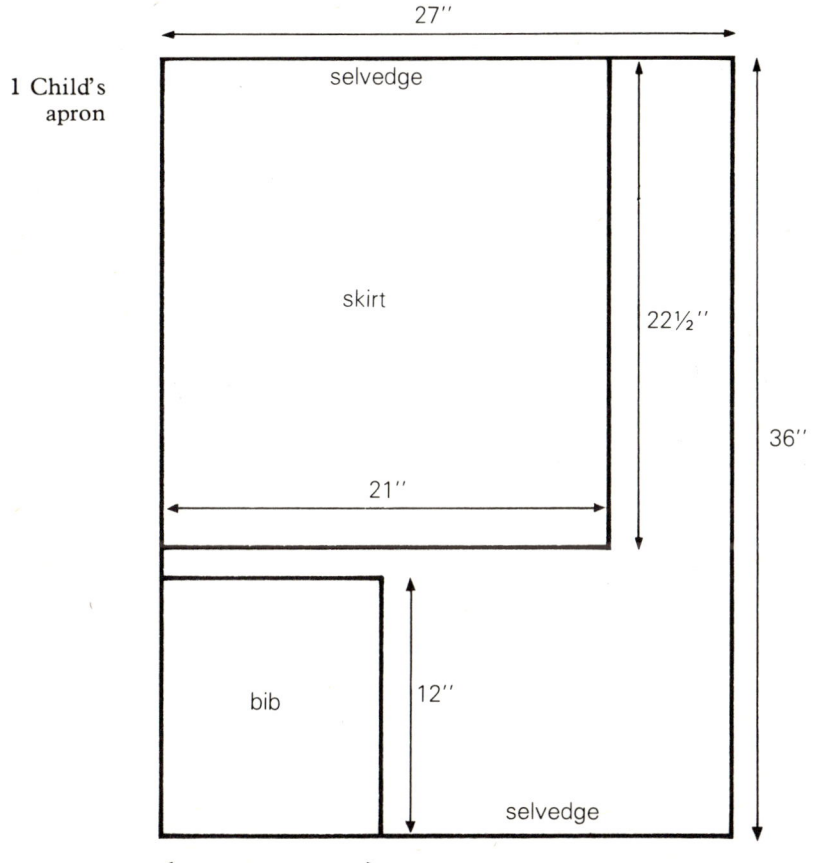

1 Child's apron

Aprons

2 Across the small rectangle (the bib) pin and then stitch two 10¼" strips of lime ribbon, ⅜" apart and 3¼" from the top edge, that is, the edge opposite the selvedge. Similarly pin and stitch a 21" length of pale blue ribbon across the large rectangle (the skirt) 5½" from the selvedge edge.

3 Neaten the sides of both the bib and skirt pieces by turning them under ¼" twice to form a hem. Tack and stitch. With a ½" overlap, pin the bib onto the skirt and sew in place with a double row of stitching.

4 For the vertical strips, cut one piece of lime ribbon 34" long and one piece of pale blue ribbon the same length, and pin them ⅛" apart on the full length of the apron, 6½" from the left-hand hemmed edge of the skirt.

5 Fold the top of the bib under ½" and then under again 1" to form a hem. Tack and stitch down. Make a similar 1½" hem at the bottom edge of the apron skirt.

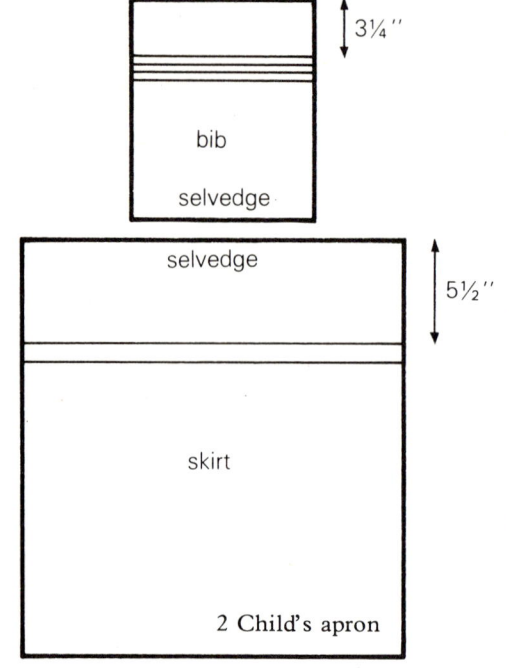

2 Child's apron

3 Child's Apron

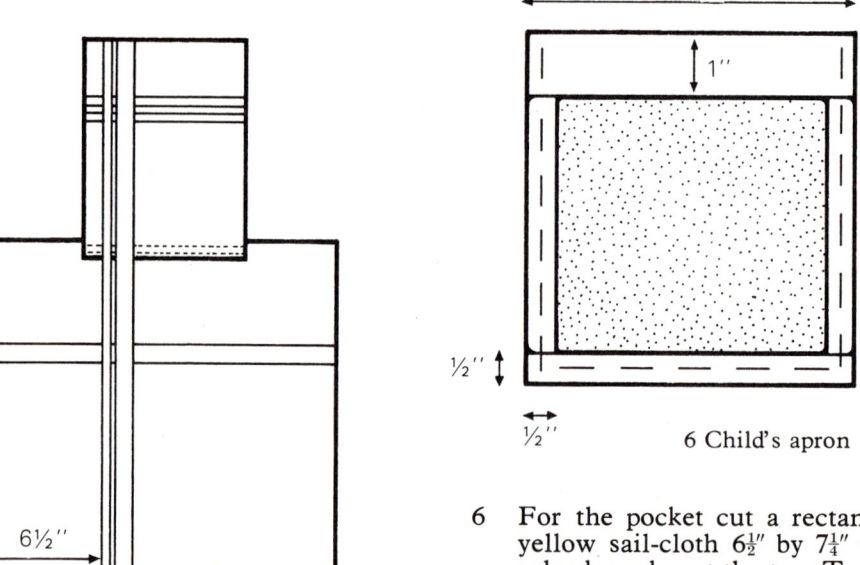

6 Child's apron

6 For the pocket cut a rectangle of yellow sail-cloth 6½" by 7¼" with a selvedge edge at the top. Turn and tack a ½" hem down the two sides and across the bottom, and a 1" hem at the top selvedge edge.

Aprons

7 Pin the tacked pocket onto the apron skirt in the lower right-hand rectangle. It should be equidistant from the hemmed edge of the apron and the vertical pale blue ribbon, and the top of the pocket should be $2\frac{1}{2}''$ from the horizontal pale blue ribbon. Stitch it in place as close to the edge as possible, making two tiny triangles of stitches at the top corners for added strength.

8 At the top edge of the skirt piece, on either side of the bib, make two outward facing $\frac{3}{8}''$ pleats $\frac{3}{4}''$ apart. Secure each one with two horizontal lines of tacking stitches.

8 Child's apron

9 Cut a 54" length of yellow ribbon for the waistband, turn the ends under $\frac{1}{4}''$ twice, and secure with hemming stitch. Pin the waistband ribbon onto the apron and tack and stitch it in position, with the ribbon aligning with the top of the apron skirt.

10 For the neckband cut a 16" piece of yellow ribbon. Cut the ends diagonally as shown and fold each over $\frac{1}{2}''$ onto the right side, trimming away any ribbon that extends beyond the side.

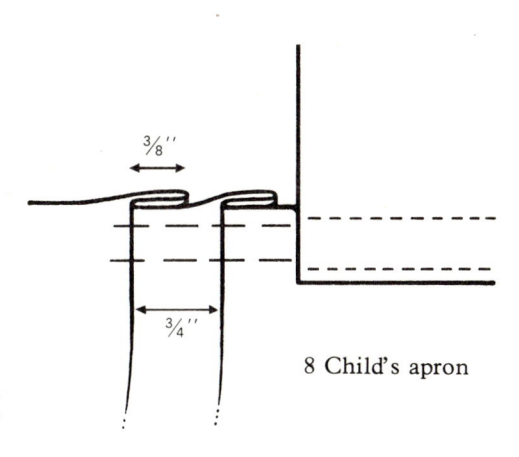

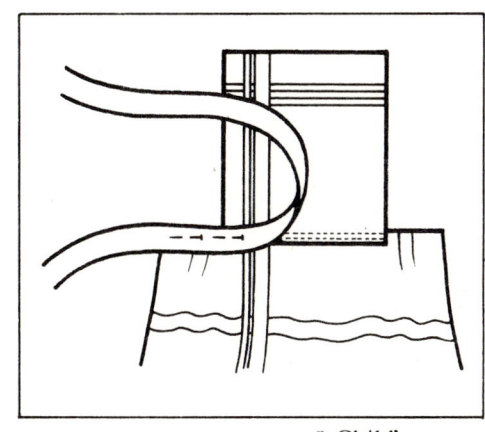

9 Child's apron

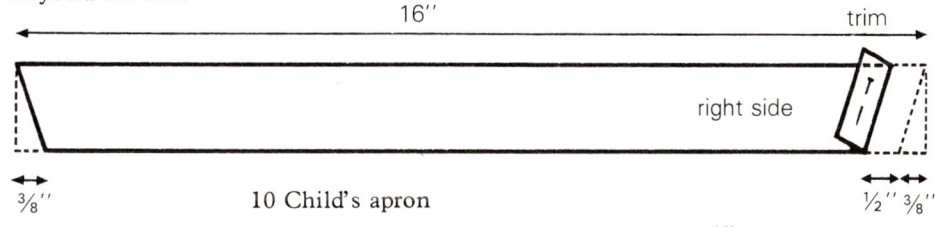

10 Child's apron

11 Over the $\frac{1}{2}''$ fold at the right-hand end of the neckband sew a 1" strip of $1\frac{1}{2}''$ wide yellow sail-cloth with $\frac{1}{4}''$ hemmed edges. This small piece of material makes a strong base for the two snap fasteners.

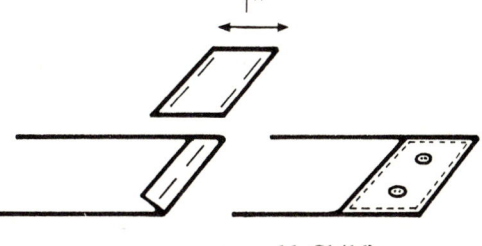

11 Child's apron

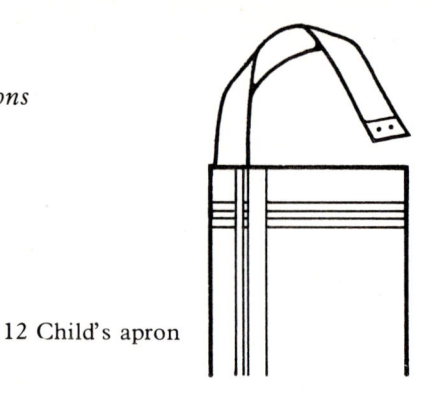

Aprons

12 Child's apron

12 Pin the left-hand end of the neckband under the top of the bib and stitch in place. Sew two snap fasteners (snappers or poppers) at the right-hand side of the neckband and at the top right inside edge of the bib.

Pinafore

Materials
2 yards mauve and white gingham 36" wide
4¾ yards pink ribbon ¼" wide
3¾ yards mauve ribbon 2" wide

1. Cut a 2 yard piece of gingham into four 5" strips for the shoulder straps and bottom frill, four 2½" strips for the waistband, and one 34½" piece for the skirt. From the remaining 7½" strip cut two pieces 7½" by 6½" for the pockets and a piece 19½" long for the bib.

2. Across the bib piece pin and tack two double rows of pink ribbon. One double row should be ⅝" below the centre and the other 1⅛" from the raw edge at the base of the rectangle. Stitch along both edges of each piece of ribbon, and remove the tacking.

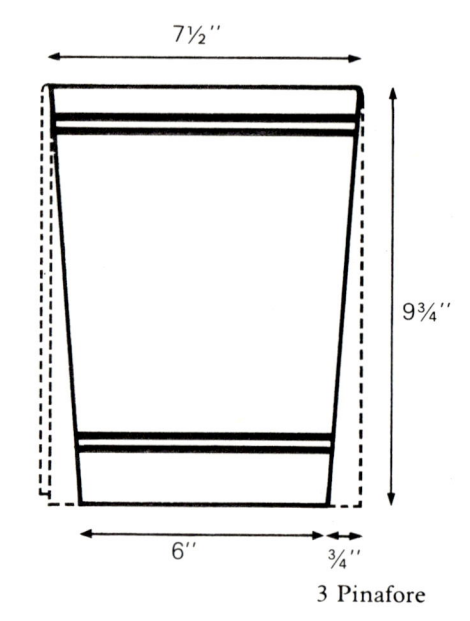

3. Fold the bib in half and trim the sides diagonally so that the folded top remains 7½" wide while the base becomes 6" wide.

3 Pinafore

2 Pinafore

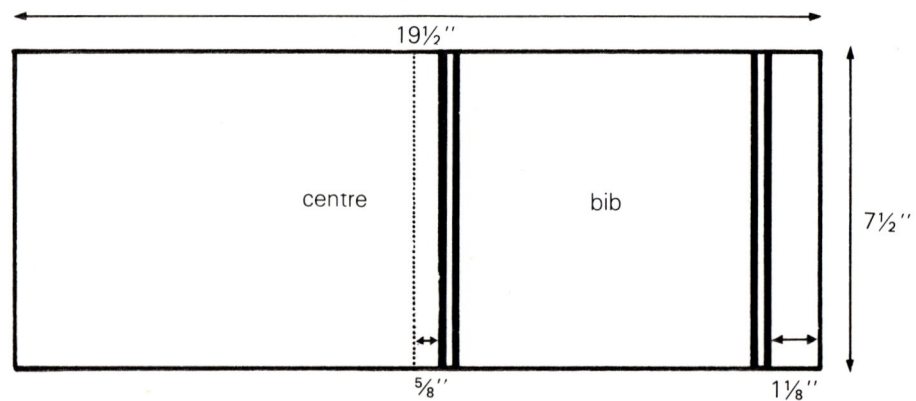

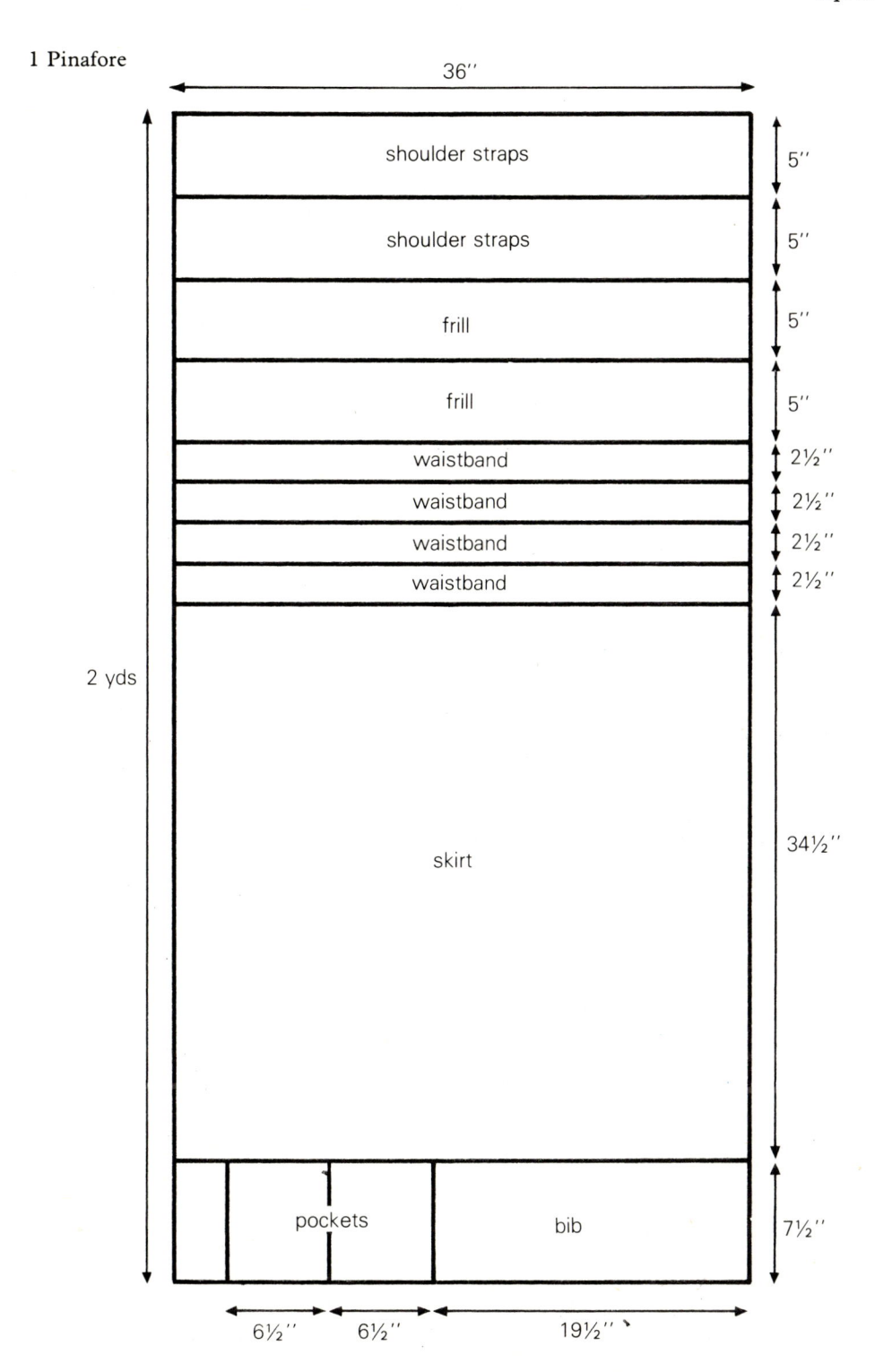

Aprons

1 Pinafore

	36"	
	shoulder straps	5"
	shoulder straps	5"
	frill	5"
	frill	5"
	waistband	2½"
	waistband	2½"
	waistband	2½"
	waistband	2½"
2 yds	skirt	34½"
	pockets / bib	7½"
	6½" / 6½" / 19½"	

63

Aprons

4 Take two of the 5″ wide gingham strips for the shoulder straps, fold both in half along their length with wrong sides together, and turn the raw edges under $\frac{1}{2}″$, holding each side in place with pins.

5 Slip $\frac{1}{2}″$ of the raw diagonal edges of the bib piece between the turned edges of the shoulder straps and pin in position. At each side tack the bib in place and continue the tacking stitches to join the sides of the shoulder straps together. Sew close to the edge and remove all tacking.

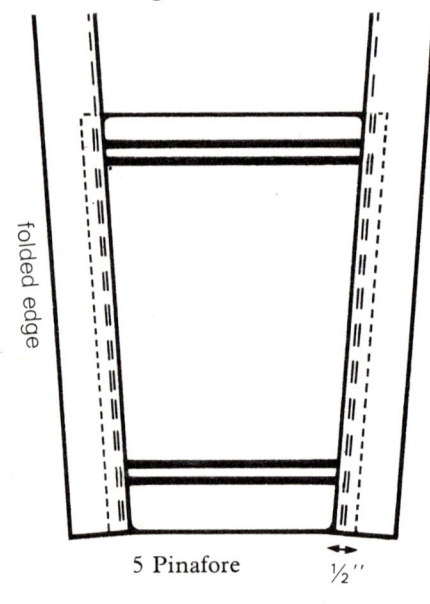

6 For the frill at the base of the skirt, join the two remaining 5″ strips of gingham together (allowing a $\frac{1}{2}″$ seam) to form a long piece 71″ by 5″. Stitch a double row of pink ribbon along the bottom of the strip, $\frac{1}{4}″$ apart and $1\frac{1}{8}″$ from the raw edge. Turn a double $\frac{1}{4}″$ hem at the edge. Along the opposite edge make two rows of running stiches $\frac{1}{8}″$ apart and $\frac{3}{4}″$ from the edge and draw the material up to 36″—about half its original length.

7 Turn one 36″ edge of the apron skirt under $\frac{1}{2}″$ and secure with tacking stitches. Pin this edge $\frac{1}{4}″$ over the frilled strip, making sure that the gathers are evenly spaced. Tack and stitch the frill in place, remove all tacking and gathering stitches, and oversew (overcast) the raw edges at the back. Turn a $\frac{1}{4}″$ hem at both sides of the skirt and along the bottom of the frill and stitch down.

8 Sew a double row of pink ribbon $\frac{1}{4}″$ apart and $2\frac{1}{8}″$ from the top edge onto both of the $7\frac{1}{2}″$ by $6\frac{1}{2}″$ pocket pieces. Fold the sides and bottom edges under $\frac{1}{2}″$ and tack in place. Turn the top edge of each pocket under $\frac{1}{2}″$ and then under 1″, tack, and stitch down.

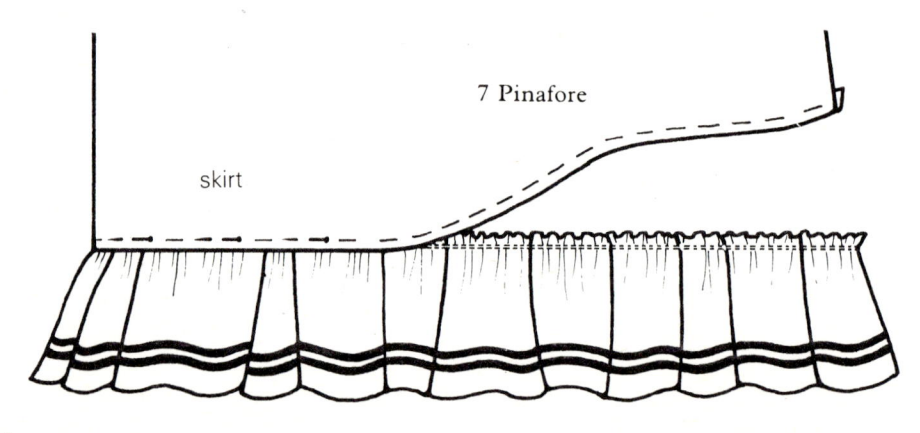

5 Pinafore $\frac{1}{2}″$

folded edge

7 Pinafore

skirt

Aprons

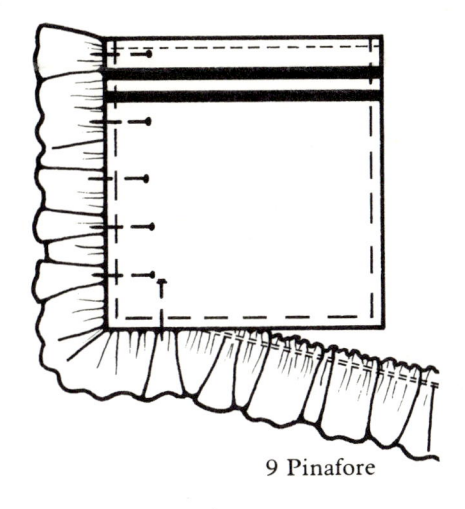

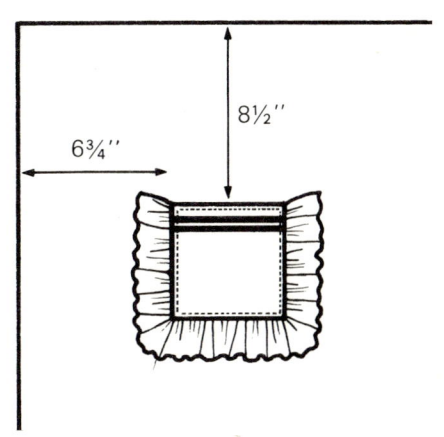

9 Pinafore

10 Pinafore: position of left-hand pocket

9   For the frills around the pockets, cut two 33" lengths of mauve ribbon. Neaten the ends of the ribbons with narrow hand-stitched hems. Down one side of each ribbon make two rows of running stitches $\frac{1}{8}$" apart and $\frac{1}{4}$" from the edge. Gather the ribbon to about half its original length and pin and tack it firmly to the back of the pocket along the sides and bottom, allowing a $\frac{3}{8}$" overlap.

10 Pin the pockets to the skirt, $8\frac{1}{2}$" from the top and $6\frac{3}{4}$" from each hemmed side. Tack them in place and stitch close to the edge. Remove all tacking and gathering stitches.

11 Make a double row of running stitches at the top of the skirt for the gathers at the waist but do not draw up the threads at this stage. Mark the centre of the top of the skirt with a pin.

12 For the waistband, join the four $2\frac{1}{2}$" wide gingham strips together in pairs (allow a $\frac{1}{2}$" seam) to make two strips 71" by $2\frac{1}{2}$". Fold all the edges under $\frac{1}{2}$" and pin and tack down. With pins, mark positions $8\frac{1}{2}$" either side of the centre seam of one of the strips.

13 Take this strip and match and pin its centre seam with the pin at the centre top edge of the skirt and

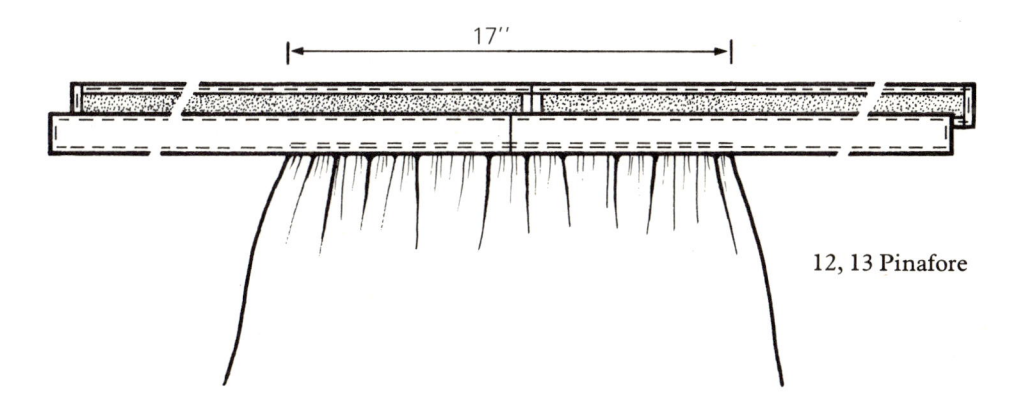

12, 13 Pinafore

65

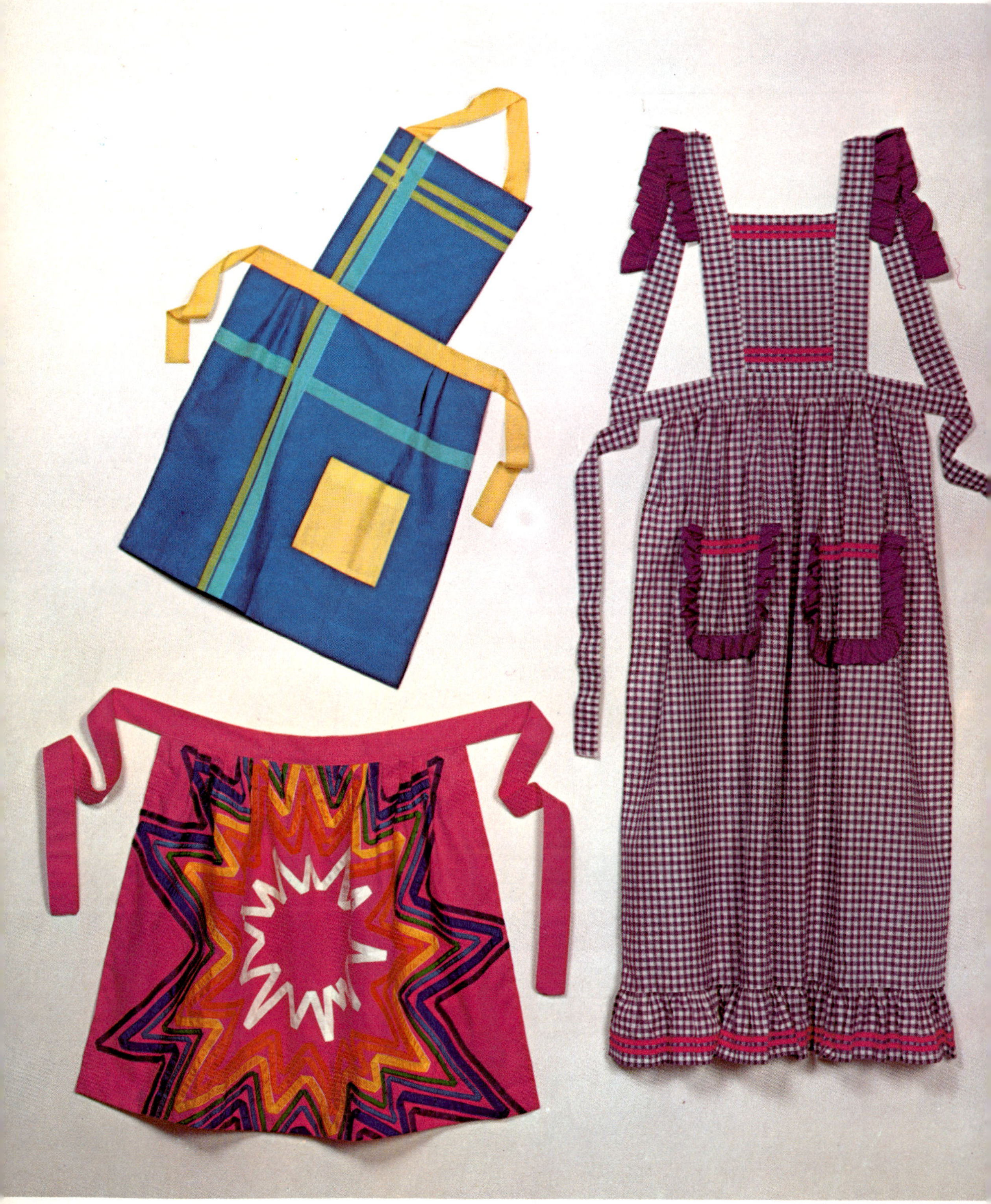

Aprons

the two side pins with the skirt sides, overlapping the top edge of the skirt $\frac{1}{2}''$ with the waistband. Draw up the gathering stitches at the top of the skirt to 17" and pin the gathered skirt edge under the waistband, ensuring that the gathers are evenly spaced. Tack in place.

14 Place the remaining waistband piece at the back of the apron, matching the centre seams so that the gathered edge of the skirt is enclosed between inner and outer waistbands. Tack the sides and bottom edges of the two waistband pieces together but leave the top open for the bib and shoulder straps.

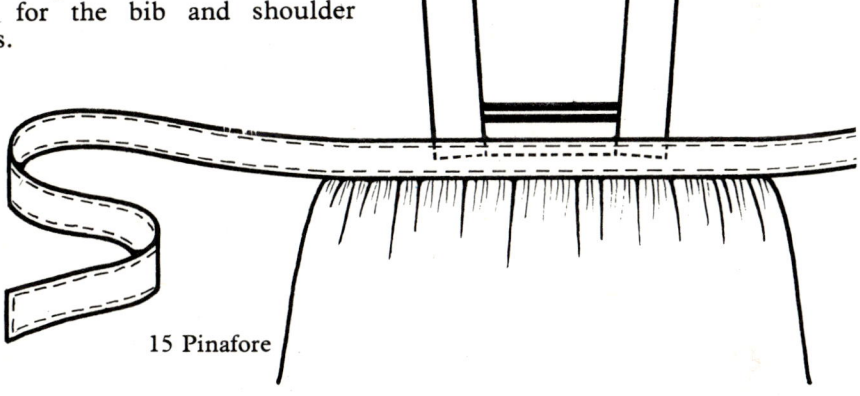

15 Insert the bib section between the inner and outer waistbands and above the middle of the apron, and tack into position.

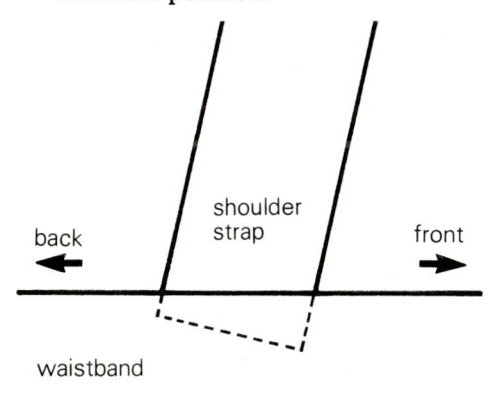

16 Try the pinafore on with the waistband tied, and adjust the length of the shoulder straps so that they fit comfortably. Between the two waistband sections at the back pin the adjusted shoulder straps in place at a slight angle as shown, leaving a space of about $6\frac{1}{2}''$ between the straps at the front and back of the pinafore.

15 Pinafore

17 Tack the top of the waistband pieces together and then stitch all round it close to the edge. Remove all tacking.

18 Finally cut two 30" long pieces of mauve ribbon for the shoulder frills, and make narrow hems at the ends. Gather the ribbons with two rows of running stitch at one edge and draw up so that the frills measure 15". Pin them under the outer edges of the shoulder straps and position so that they set centrally over the shoulder. Tack and stitch the frills in place and remove any remaining tacking and gathering stitches.

16 Pinafore: angling the shoulder straps

Child's bolero

The measurements given are for a girl of 7 to 8 years old, but different sizes can be made by copying the pattern onto a piece of paper divided into smaller or larger squares than one inch. The amount of ribbon required for each frill is a little over one-and-a-half times the full width of the bolero.

Materials
Sheet of paper 20″ by 18″ divided into one inch squares
1 yard material (nylon or rayon) for the bolero 36″ wide
$\frac{1}{2}$ yard interfacing 36″ wide
$9\frac{1}{2}$ yards green ribbon $1\frac{1}{2}$″ wide
8 yards red ribbon $1\frac{1}{2}$″ wide
1 yard red ribbon $\frac{1}{4}$″ wide

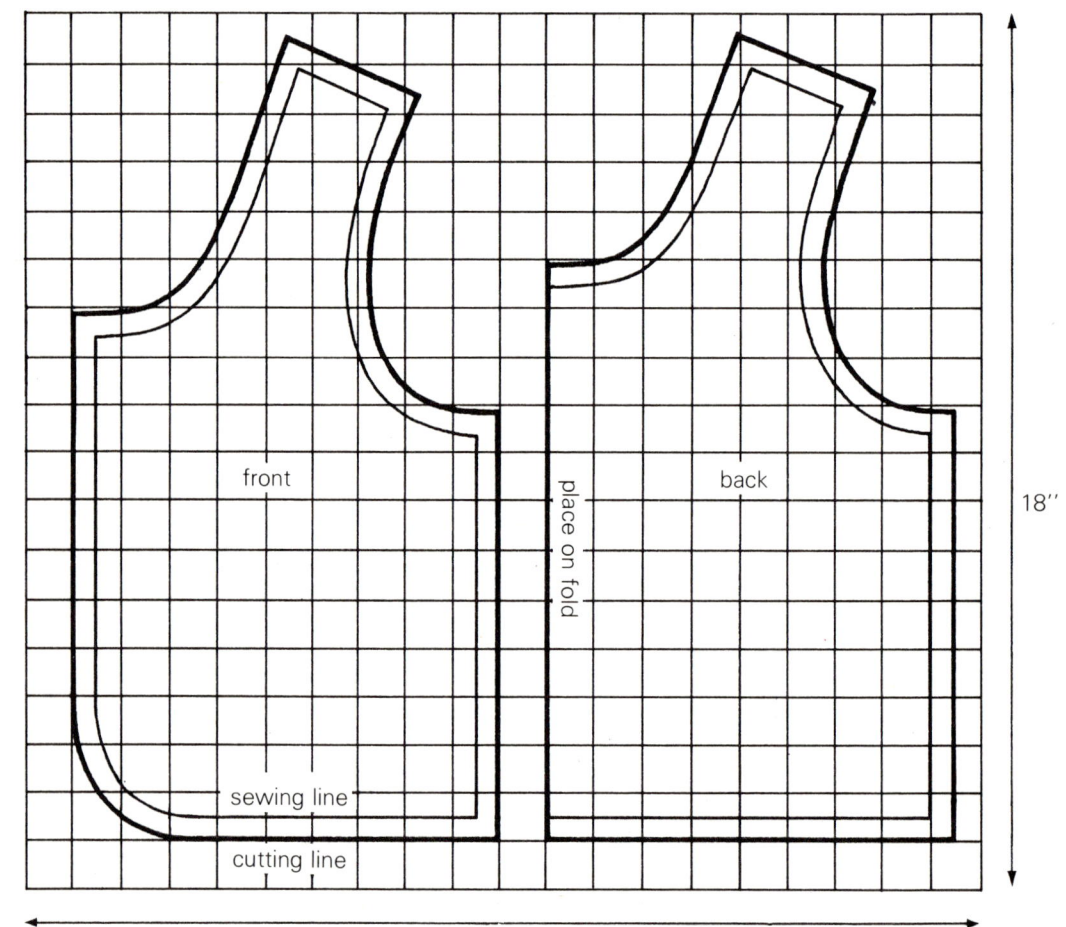

1 Child's bolero: drawing the pattern onto squared paper

1 Copy the pattern from the diagram onto a sheet of paper divided into one inch squares and cut it out.

Child's bolero

2 Fold the bolero material in half, and using the paper pattern, cut out two sets of pieces. The back should be placed against the fold and the front away from the fold both times — this will give four front pieces and two back pieces. Similarly, from the folded interfacing cut out two front pieces and one back piece. Pin, tack, and sew all the side seams, making three pieces — one outside, one lining (the same material as the outside), and one interfacing. Allow $\frac{1}{2}"$ for all the seams.

3 Pin the interfacing onto the wrong side of the lining. With right sides facing inwards, pin the outside and the lining plus interfacing together, leaving a gap at least 4" wide at the bottom centre back (so that the garment can be turned the right way out). Tack and sew together. Remove tacking and trim the seams and corners and clip the curves.

3 Child's bolero

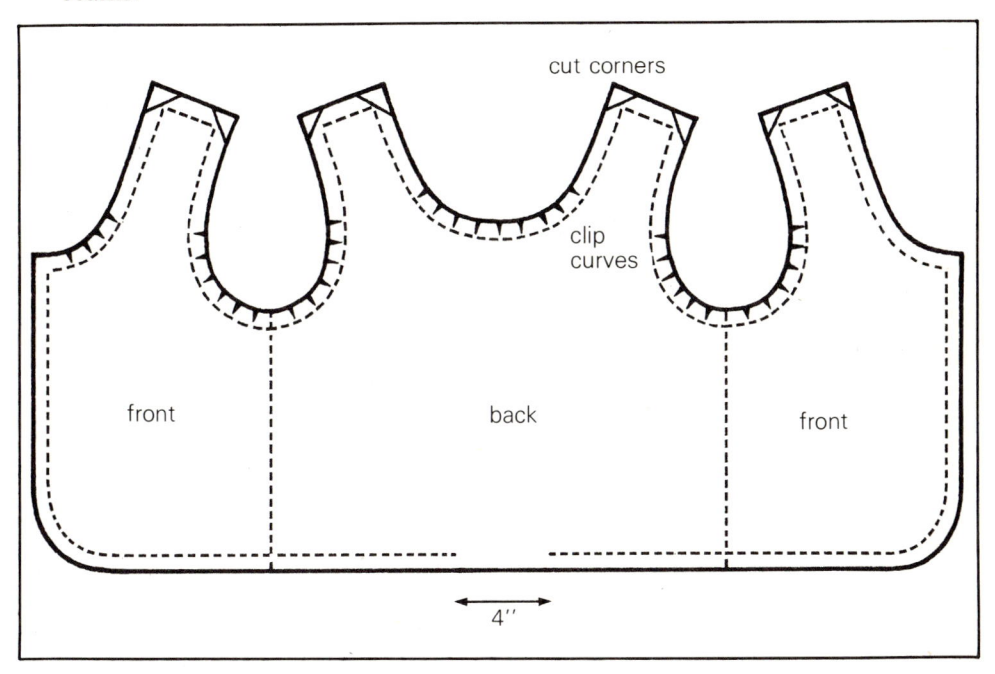

4 Turn the garment the right way out and oversew (overcast) the shoulder seams and the 4" gap at the bottom. Press the bolero.

5 Cut six pieces of the wide green ribbon 50" long and five pieces of red ribbon 50" long. Turn the ends under $\frac{1}{4}"$ twice and secure with small running stitches.

6 Gather one of the green ribbons with small running stitches close to one edge to about 32". Pin the ribbon along the bottom of the bolero $\frac{1}{2}"$ up from the edge. Tack it in place and then machine stitch it very close to the gathered edge. Remove tacking and gathering stitches.

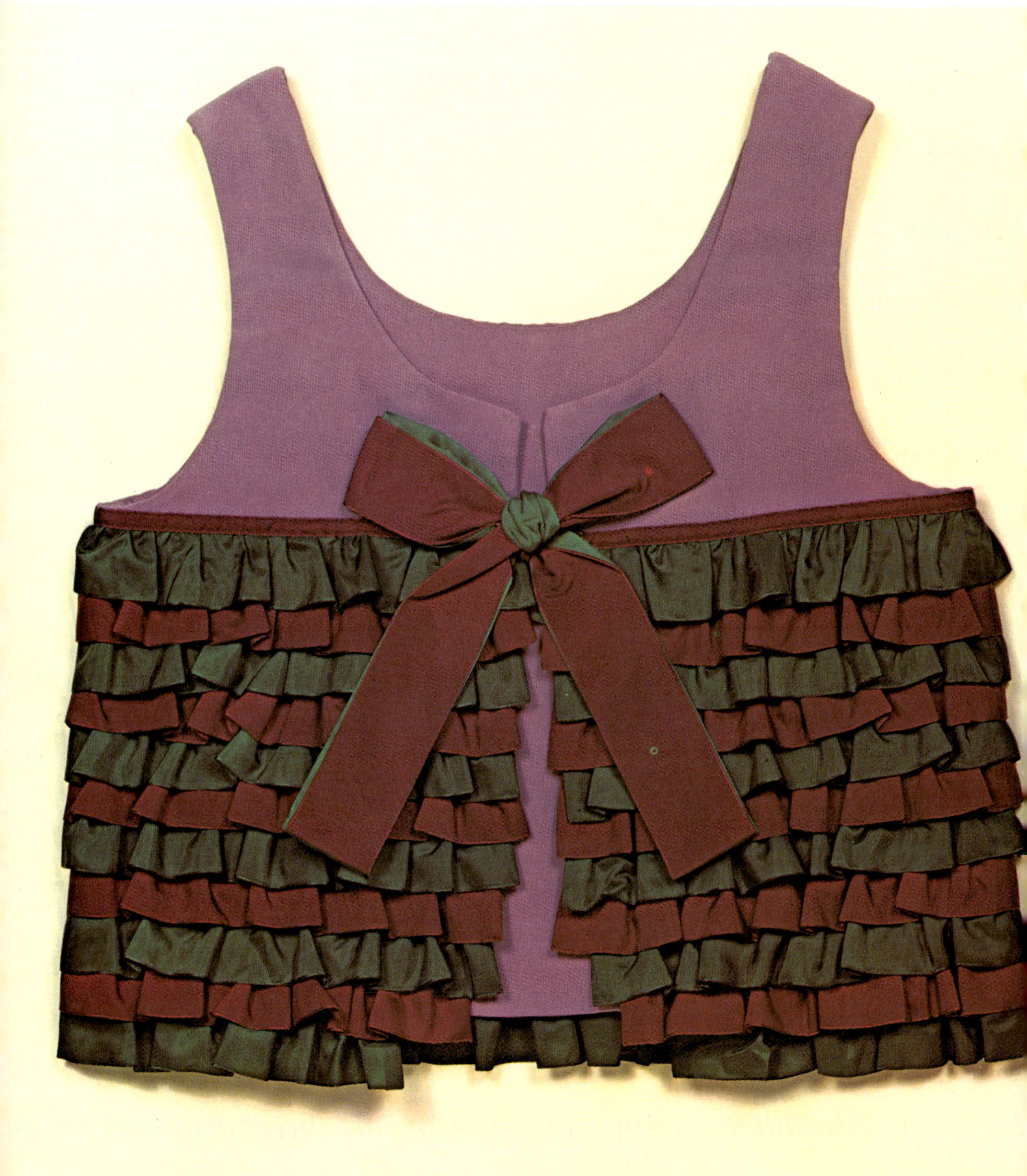

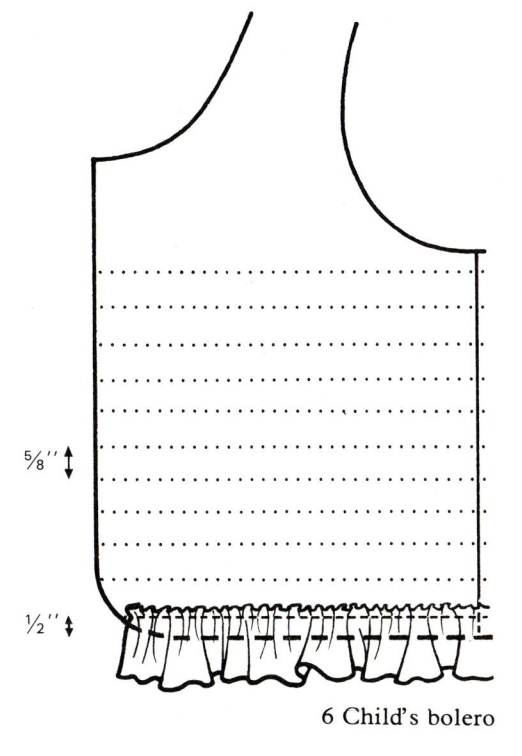

Child's bolero

7 Pin a piece of gathered red ribbon $\frac{5}{8}"$ above the first green one, and tack and stitch it in place. Continue adding layers of gathered ribbon in alternate colours $\frac{5}{8}"$ above the previous layer until all eleven lengths have been sewn on, removing tacking and gathering stitches each time.

8 Cover the final layer with a piece of the narrow red ribbon $32\frac{1}{2}"$ long, and turn the ends under $\frac{1}{4}"$.

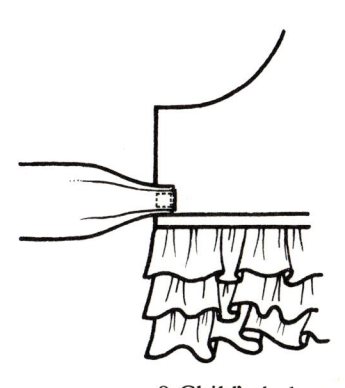

6 Child's bolero

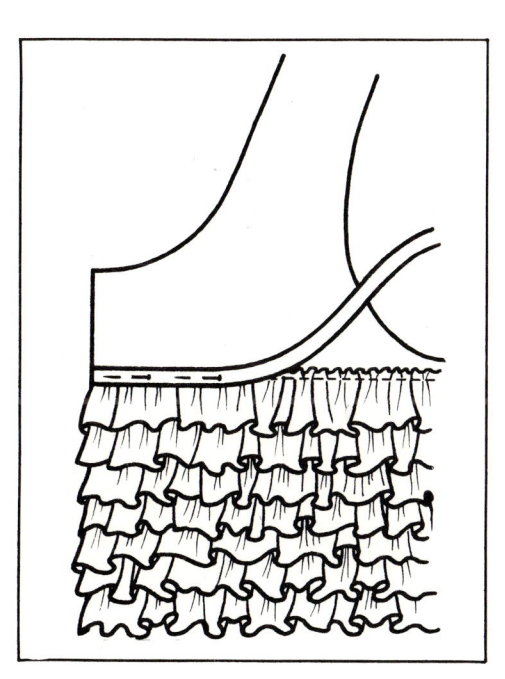

9 Child's bolero

9 For the bow, cut four 18" lengths of ribbon, two red and two green. Place one red and one green one together and fold the ends over $\frac{1}{4}"$. Then make a gathering-type fold in order to reduce the width of the ribbon end. Pin the folded end onto the left front of the bolero just above the frilled ribbons and stitch firmly in position.

10 Repeat this process with the other two ribbons for the right side of the bolero. Neaten all the raw ends with a tiny hem or a V cut into the centre to prevent fraying.

8 Child's bolero

Embroidered box

Canvas embroidery using ribbons instead of wool produces a very rich effect but unfortunately it requires rather a large amount of ribbon (approximately 1 yard for 54 stitches) which can of course be expensive, so it is preferable to make small objects; for example, a purse, a spectacle case or, as illustrated, the lid of a box. For more practical purposes, the box could be lined with plastic instead of material.

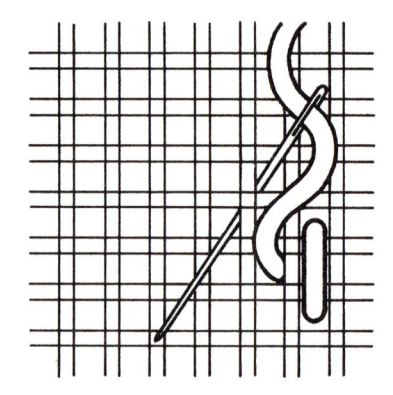

Materials
Piece of double-weave canvas $9\frac{1}{2}''$ by 7" (10 holes per square inch)
Blunt needle with a large eye
12 yards maroon ribbon $\frac{1}{4}''$ wide
$6\frac{1}{2}$ yards apricot ribbon $\frac{1}{4}''$ wide
$6\frac{1}{2}$ yards pink ribbon $\frac{1}{4}''$ wide
$4\frac{1}{2}$ yards red ribbon $\frac{1}{4}''$ wide
$4\frac{1}{2}$ yards cream ribbon $\frac{1}{4}''$ wide
$2\frac{1}{2}$ yards orange ribbon $\frac{1}{4}''$ wide
Sheet of strong cardboard (not too thick) for the box
$\frac{1}{2}$ yard maroon taffeta or satin material 36" wide
2 yards braid or cord for edging about $\frac{3}{16}''$ wide

The lid
1 The type of stitch used in the design is based on a Florentine stitch, and is worked vertically in a diagonal line over two double threads of canvas and one hole. When commencing stitching do not tie knots in the ribbon but weave any loose ends under other worked stitches. Keep the tension of the stitches even and do not draw the ribbon up too tightly or the canvas will buckle.

2 In the design illustrated, each square represents one stitch, that is, one hole of canvas (see stitch diagram). From this design, find the centre point of the canvas and work all the maroon stitching. Fol-

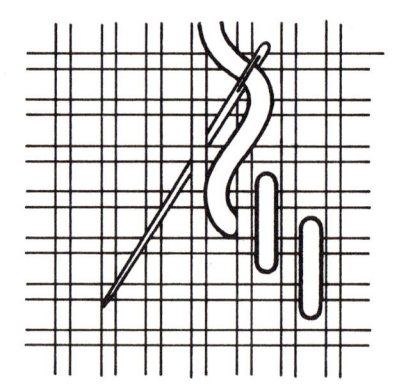

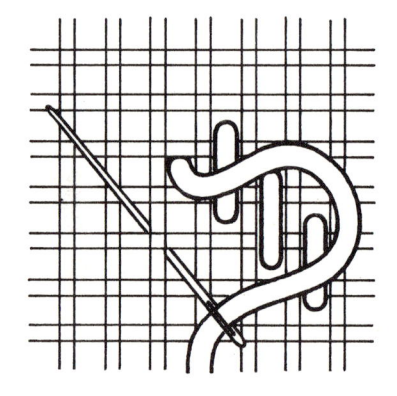

1 Lid: Florentine stitch

lowing the pattern, complete the design using each coloured ribbon in turn.

72

Embroidered box

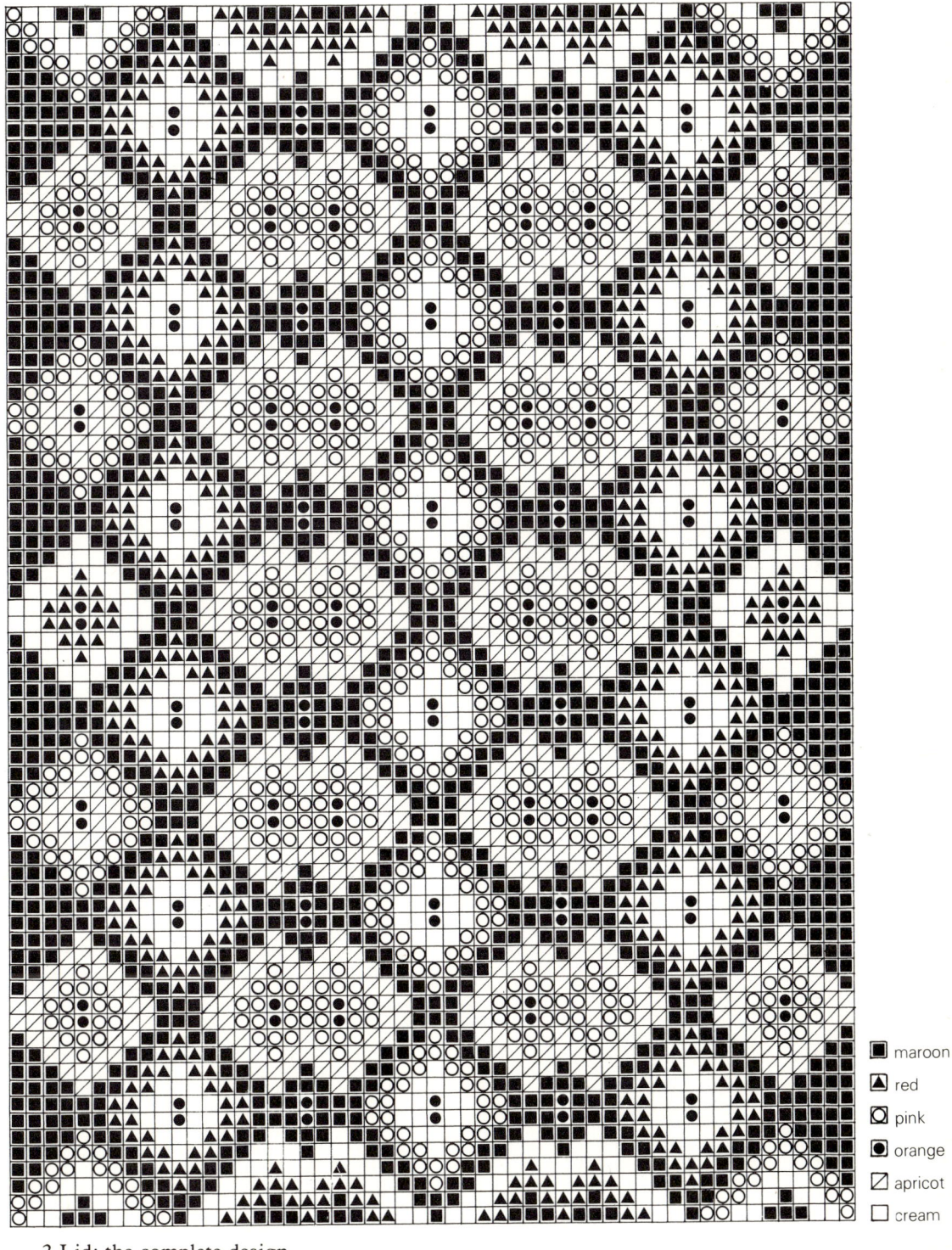

■ maroon
▲ red
◉ pink
● orange
◹ apricot
☐ cream

2 Lid: the complete design

The box
1. Cut six rectangles of cardboard: two pieces 7¾" by 2½", two pieces 7¾" by 5¼", and two pieces 5⅛" by 2½". For each rectangle, excepting the lid (one of the 7¾" by 5¼" pieces) which will only require one, cut two pieces of taffeta or satin material 1" longer and 1" wider than the cardboard.

2. Place one of the rectangles of cardboard centrally on the wrong side of one of the corresponding pieces of material. Turn the edges of the material over the cardboard, and lace the sides and the top and bottom together with large diagonal stitches, turning the corners under.

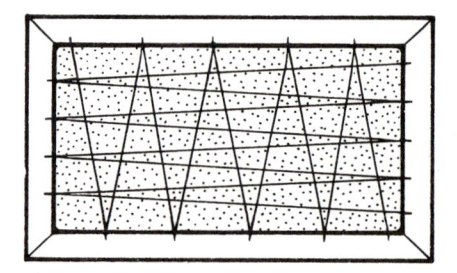

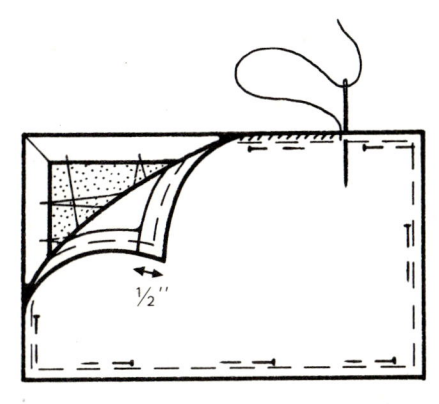

Drawstring bag

3 Box

5 Place the two long sides onto the base section and oversew (overcast) them along the outside edge. Sew the two ends onto the base and sides, and then attach the lid with oversewing (overcasting) stitches along one side only to form the hinge.

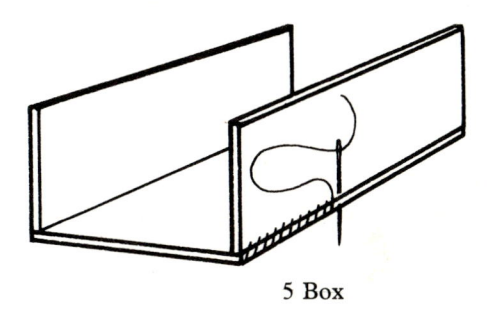

5 Box

3 Tack a ½" hem around the second piece. Oversew (overcast) this onto the first piece, covering the lacing stitches. Remove tacking. Cover the other four rectangles, except the lid, in the same way.

4 Stretch the worked canvas over the cardboard lid, being careful not to buckle it, and secure it at the back with lacing stitches, sewing at least three rows of double threads in from the edge to prevent fraying. Cover the inside of the lid with material in the same way as the other rectangles.

6 At each vertical corner sew a $2\frac{3}{4}"$ strip of braid so that it covers the joining stitches of the sides. Turn the braid under ¼" at the top edge — the other end can be left raw as it will be covered by the braid around the base. Similarly sew $26\frac{1}{2}"$ lengths of braid around the lid and around the base, making both joins at the back of the box.

Drawstring bag

A basic knowledge of crochet is required to make this bag. The abbreviations used are ch. for chain, tr. for treble, ss. for slip stitch, and dc. for double crochet.

Materials
16 yards pink ribbon $\frac{3}{8}"$ wide
18 yards cream ribbon $\frac{3}{8}"$ wide
18 yards brown ribbon $\frac{3}{8}"$ wide
Nos 10 and 8 crochet hooks
¼ yard rayon lining material

Bag
With no. 10 crochet hook and using pink ribbon, make five chain stitches and join with slip stitch to form a ring.

1st round 2 ch. to stand for first tr., 2 tr., into ring, (1 ch., 3 tr., into ring) 3 times, 1 ch., ss. to top of first 2 ch. Fasten off.

75

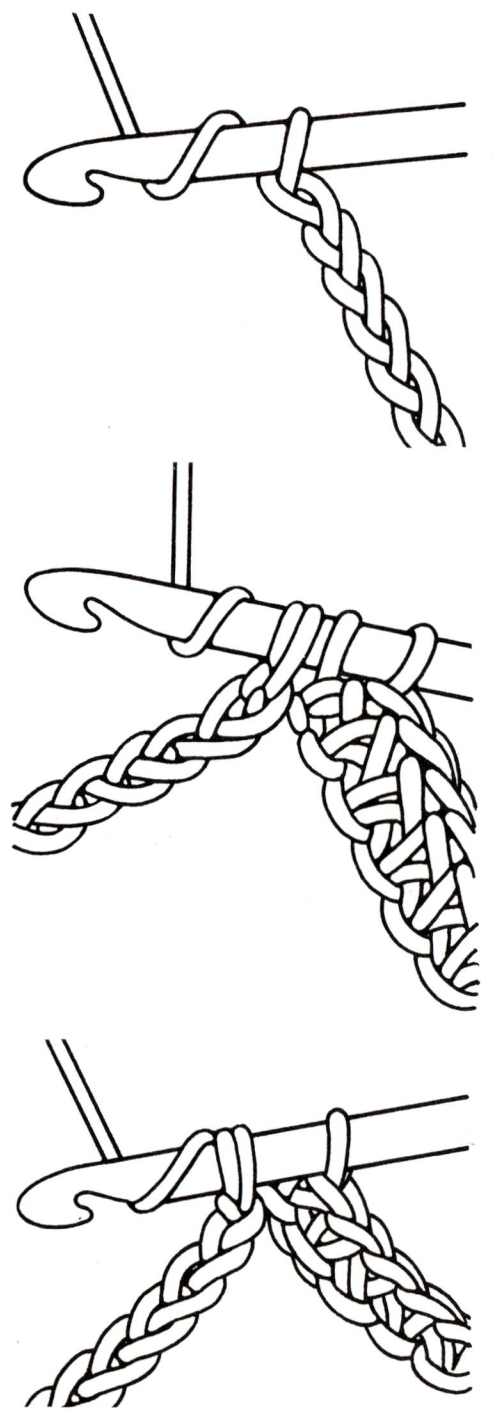

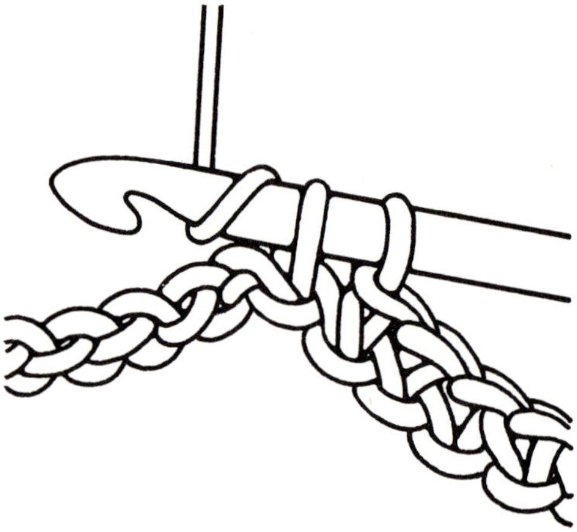

Drawstring bag

Drawstring bag: the four basic stitches

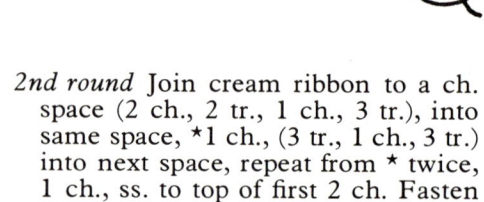

2nd round Join cream ribbon to a ch. space (2 ch., 2 tr., 1 ch., 3 tr.), into same space, *1 ch., (3 tr., 1 ch., 3 tr.) into next space, repeat from * twice, 1 ch., ss. to top of first 2 ch. Fasten off.

3rd round Rejoin pink ribbon to corner 1 ch. space (2 ch., 2 tr., 1 ch., 3 tr.), into same space, *1 ch., 3 tr., in next space, 1 ch., (3 tr., 1 ch., 3 tr.) into corner space. Repeat from * twice more, 1 ch., 3 tr. in next space, 1 ch., ss. to top of 2 ch. Fasten off.

4th round Join brown ribbon to a corner space, 1 ch., 1 dc., into a corner space. Dc. all round the square working 3 dc. in each corner. Join with ss. into first chain.

1st row 2 ch. to stand for first tr., work 1 row of tr. across 1 side of the square.

2nd row 2 ch. to stand for first tr. Miss one space, 1 tr. into next space, 1 ch., 1 tr., 1 ch. into each alternate space to the end of the row.

3rd row 1 dc. in each space to end of row. Fasten off.

4th row With no. 8 crochet hook join cream ribbon to edge. 3 ch., 1 ss. into 3rd space, *(3 ch., ss. into every other space). Repeat from * to end of row. Fasten off.

5th row Rejoin brown ribbon to opposite side of square. Using no. 10 crochet hook, 2 ch. to stand for first tr., 1 tr. into each space to end of row.

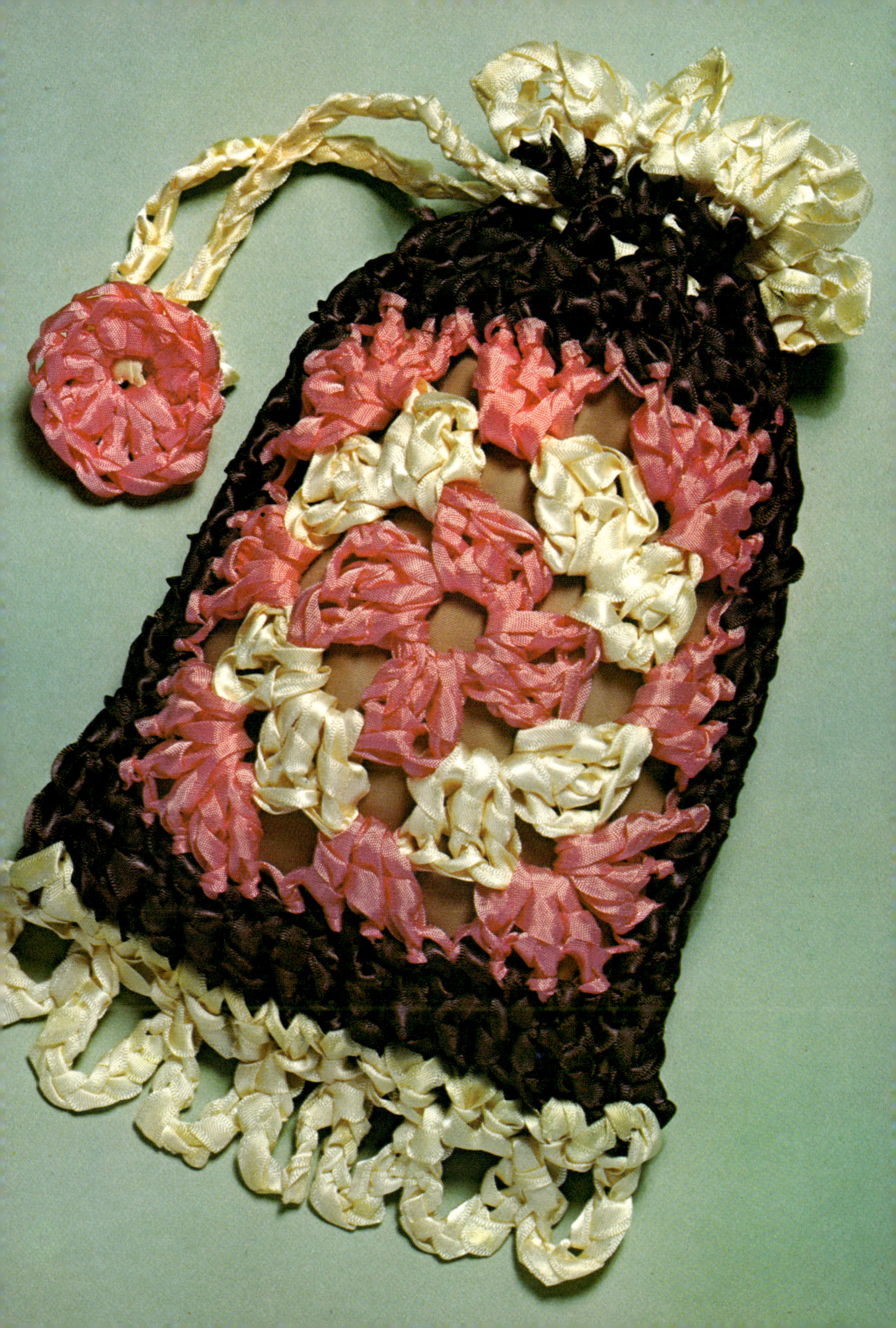

Drawn-thread tablecloth

Repeat rounds 1 to 4 and rows 1 to 5 for the other side of the bag. Join the sides of the bag with brown ribbon leaving the top and bottom open. Using no. 8 crochet hook, join the cream ribbon to the bottom corner of the bag.

1st row Join the two pieces with a row of dc.
2nd row 5 ch., ss. into third space. *(5 ch., ss. into every other space). Repeat from * to end of row. Fasten off.

Draw string
Using no. 8 crochet hook and cream ribbon, make a length of chain stitches 30" long. Thread the chain twice through the brown loops at the top of the bag. Join the ends.

Pink motif
Using no. 10 crochet hook and pink ribbon, make five chain stitches and join with slip stitch to form a ring.
1st round 2 ch. to stand for first tr., 17 tr. into ring, join to top of 2 ch. with ss. Fasten off. Sew to cream chain at join.

Lining for bag
Cut a rectangle 13" by 9" of the lining and fold it in half across its width. With right sides together, join the side seam and bottom seam, and trim them to $\frac{1}{8}$". Turn the lining inside out and stitch the seams again, enclosing the raw edges. Turn the top edge under $\frac{1}{4}$" twice and stitch. With the lining the right way out, pin it into the ribbon bag and sew in place with tiny stitches on the brown ribbon just below the draw string.

Drawn-thread tablecloth

In this traditional form of needlework, which is particularly suitable for edging tablecloths and napkins, a number of threads are pulled out of the material and the remaining threads are stitched together in groups so that the spaces and threads form a pattern. The addition of ribbon woven through the grouped threads adds colour and variety.

Materials
Piece of white, evenly-woven cotton, linen, or synthetic material, about 49" square (about 16 threads to 1")
6 yards red ribbon $\frac{7}{8}$" wide

1 At a point 2" in from a raw edge of the tablecloth material draw out a thread. Continue pulling out threads, working away from the edge, until a strip $\frac{3}{8}$" wide is made. Keep all the drawn threads for stitching.

2 Leave the next four threads and then draw out a strip $\frac{7}{8}$" wide to take the ribbon. Border this with another four threads and draw out a second $\frac{3}{8}$" wide strip.

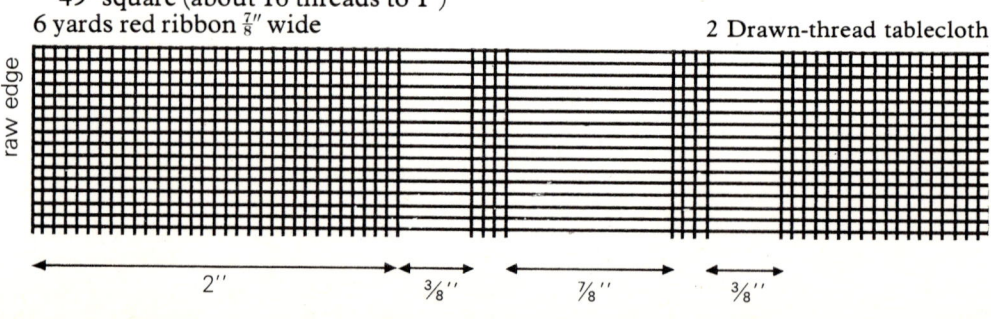

2 Drawn-thread tablecloth

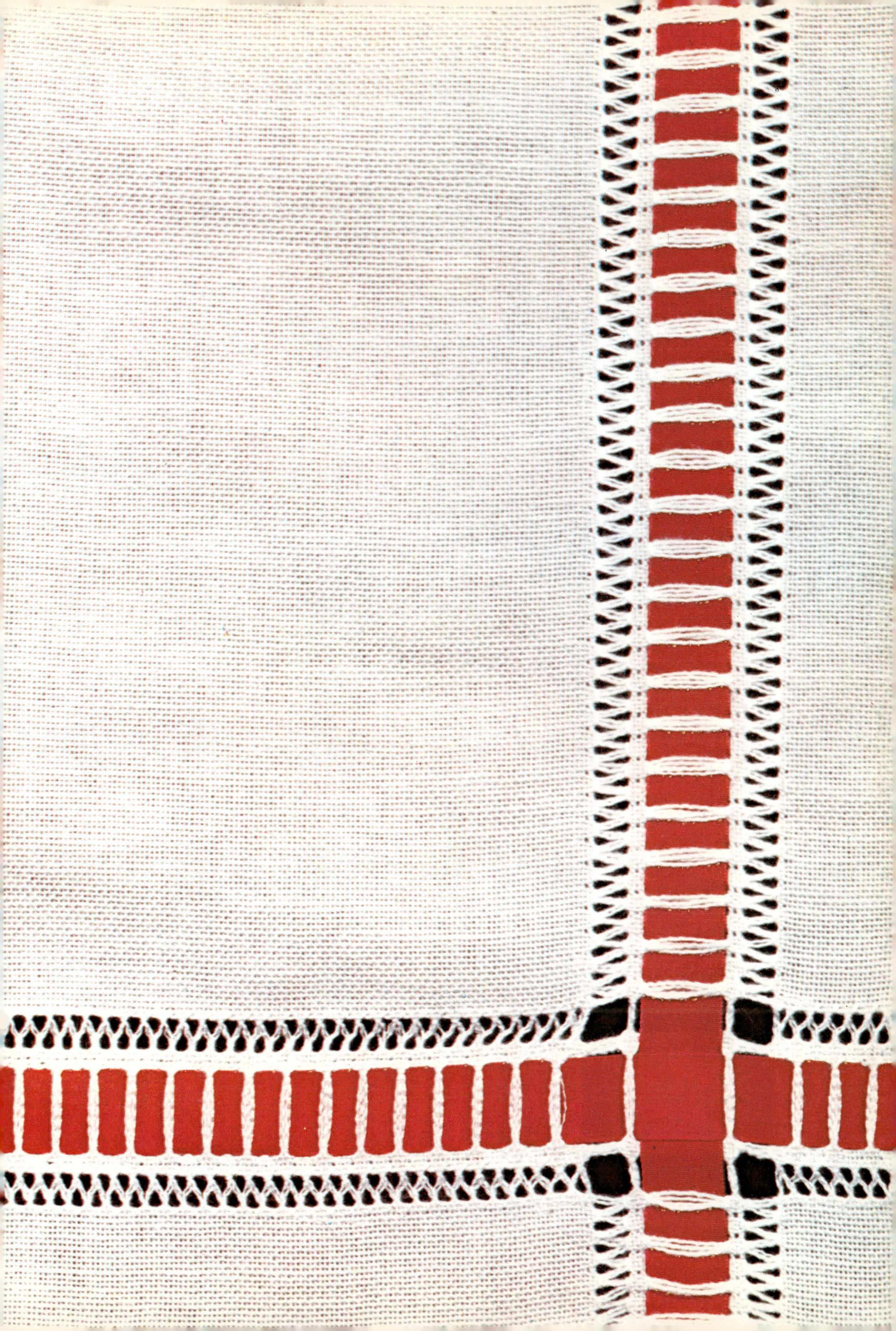

Drawn-thread tablecloth

3 Do the same along an adjacent side, but leave the other two sides for the moment. Oversew (overcast) or machine stitch the raw edges of the tablecloth to prevent them fraying while the drawn threads are worked. Along both edges of the $\frac{7}{8}''$ strips, and using the previously drawn threads, secure the threads running across the strips in groups of four with hem stitch.

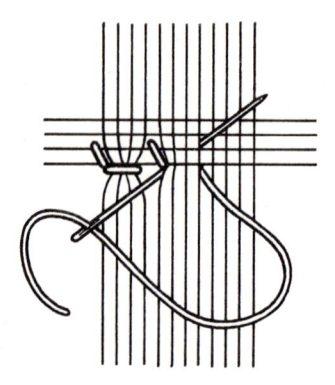

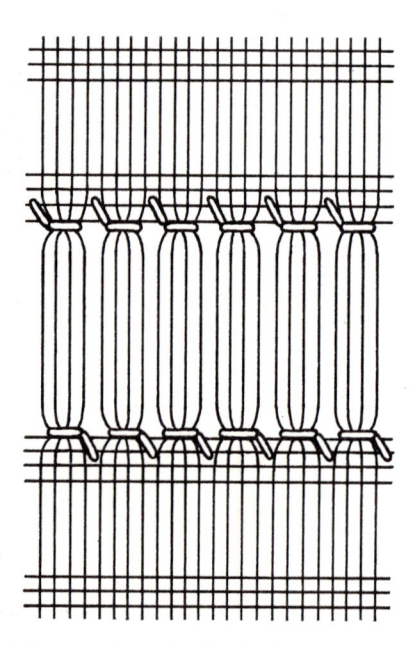

4 Repeat this process along the remaining two sides, first ensuring that the middle section of the material between the borders contains a number of threads, both warp and weft, that is divisible by four (as already grouped).

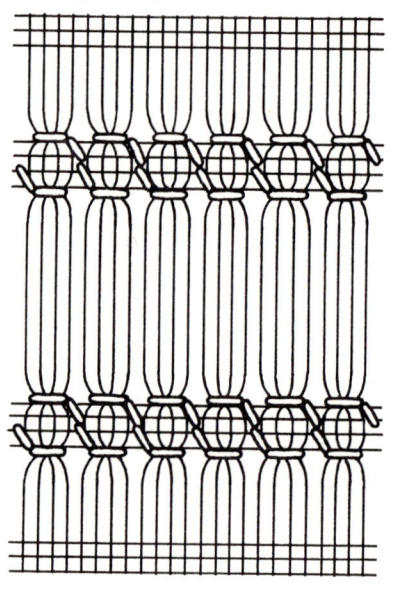

5 Drawn-thread tablecloth

3 Drawn-thread tablecloth: securing the threads in groups of four

5 Work the two inside edges of all the $\frac{3}{8}''$ strips (those bordering the $\frac{7}{8}''$ strip) into fours following the same grouping as in the $\frac{7}{8}''$ strip.

6 Along the outside edges of each $\frac{3}{8}''$ strip, hem stitch two threads of one group of four with two threads of the next, so alternating the groups and producing a zigzag effect.

7 Weave four lengths of ribbon through the four middle strips of the worked drawn threads, going above and below alternate groups. The ribbons will cross at each corner.

8 Make a hem around the tablecloth turning the edges and the ribbon ends under $\frac{1}{4}''$ twice and machine or hand stitch down.

Baby's angel top

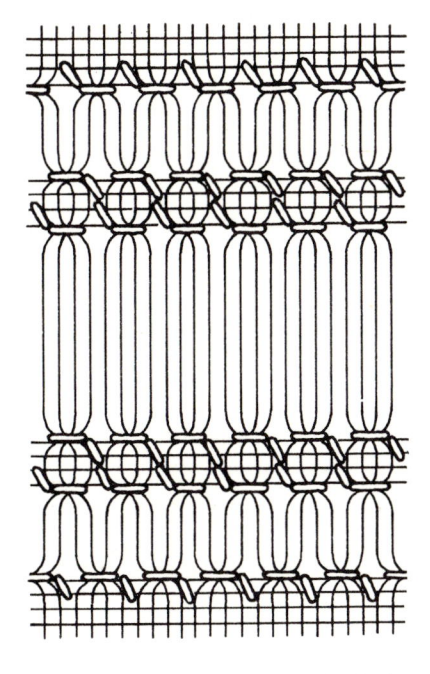

6 Drawn-thread tablecloth

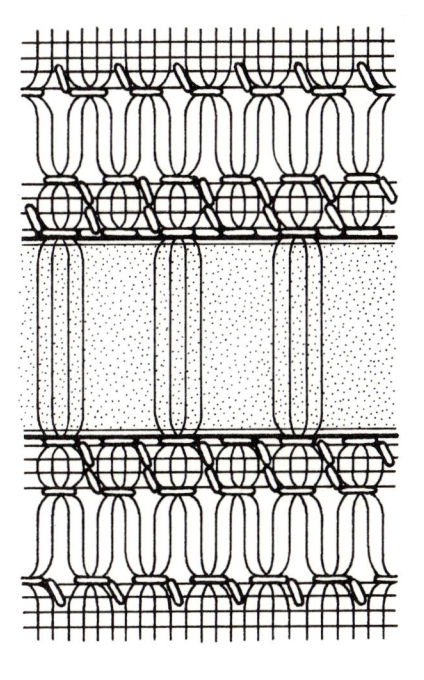

7 Drawn-thread tablecloth

Baby's angel top

A light-weight cotton material with a self-coloured woven pattern is most suitable for making this angel top, which will fit a baby of six months. Make sure that the ribbon used for the edging and decorative motifs is fully washable. By adjusting the measurements, this top could also serve as a smock for a young girl, in which case the two outer motifs could be replaced by pockets.

Materials
Sheet of paper 22″ by 28″ divided into one inch squares
1 yard light-weight white cotton 36″ wide
$\frac{3}{4}$ yard white bias binding $\frac{1}{2}$″ wide
$3\frac{1}{4}$ yards pink ribbon $\frac{1}{2}$″ wide
2 yards pink ribbon $\frac{7}{8}$″ wide
$\frac{1}{2}$ yard narrow elastic
Blunt needle with a large eye
3 white buttons $\frac{1}{4}$″ in diameter
3 pink flower motifs 1″ in diameter
Snap fastener (snapper or popper)

Baby's angel top

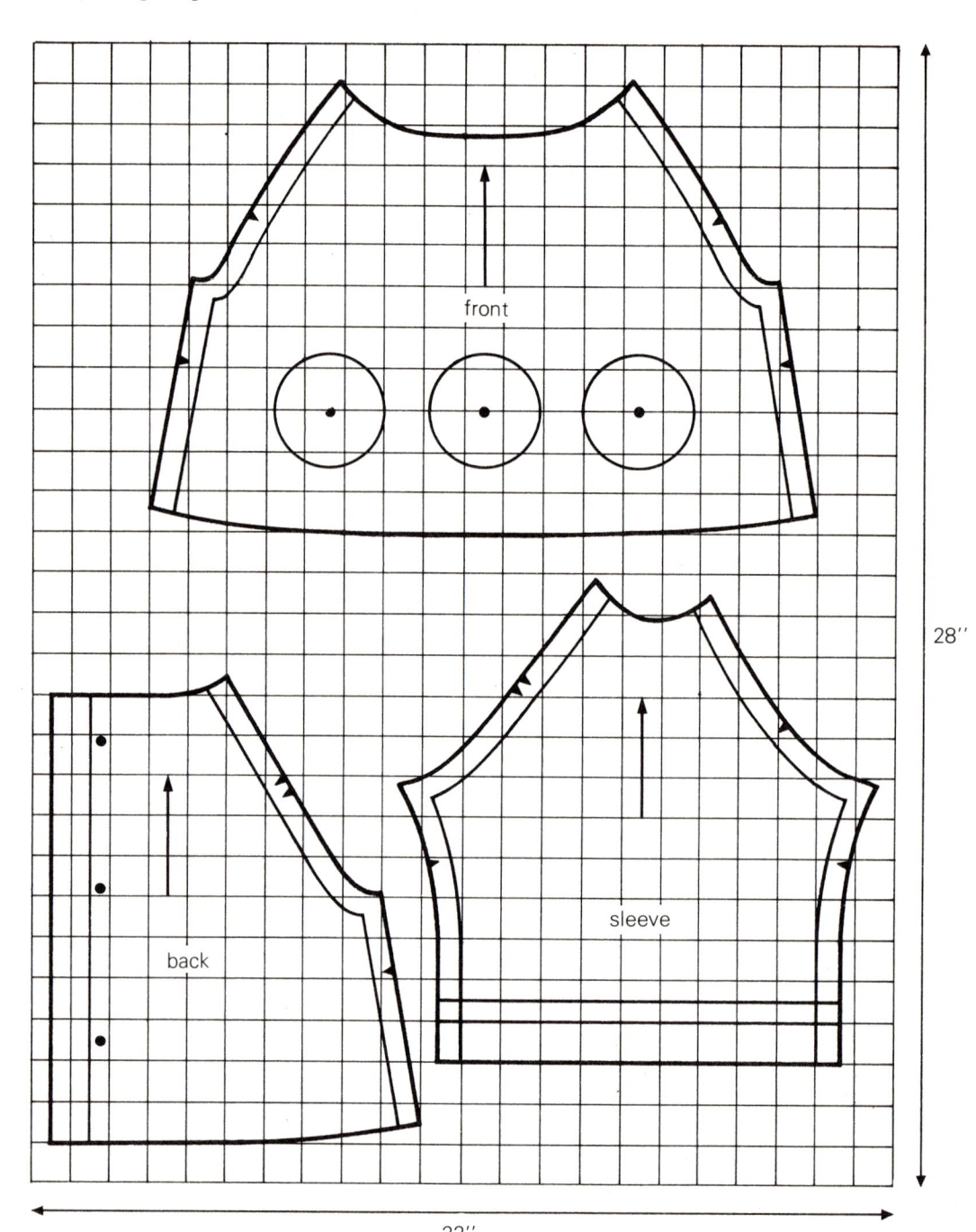

1 Baby's angel top: drawing the pattern onto squared paper

1 Copy the pattern onto a piece of paper divided into one inch squares, and cut out a front piece, two back pieces, and two sleeves. Transfer all the pattern marks onto the material.

82

Baby's angel top

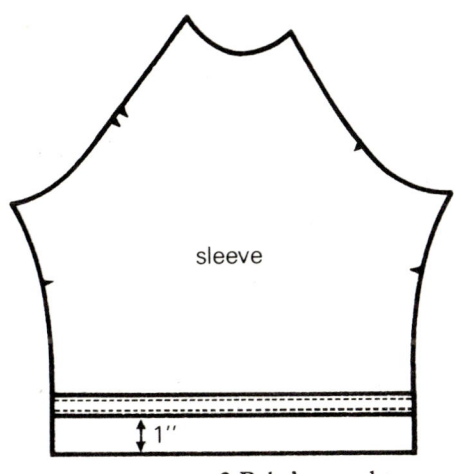

2 Baby's angel top

2. Pin a piece of white bias binding 10″ long to the inside of each sleeve 1″ from the wrist. Tack and sew the binding in place along each edge (the elastic will run through the binding).

3. Turn under a 1″ hem down the straight edge of each back piece.

4. Cut 72 pieces of ½″ wide pink ribbon 1¼″ long for the flower motifs, and fold each piece in half.

5. For each flower motif pin eight folded ribbons in a circle 2¾″ in diameter in one of the positions already marked. The raw edges should face inwards to the centre of the circle. Tack and oversew (overcast) the ribbons at the centre using a zigzag machine stitch if possible.

Baby's angel top

6 Stitch the next layer of eight ribbons in place, each 'petal' alternating with the previous round. Add a final round of ribbons and stitch in place. Cover all the zigzag stitches in the centre with a single, pink, 1" diameter flower motif, sewing this down very securely.

7 With right sides together, pin the sleeves to the front and back pieces, matching the notches, and sew together allowing a $\frac{5}{8}''$ seam. Clip the curves and press the seams.

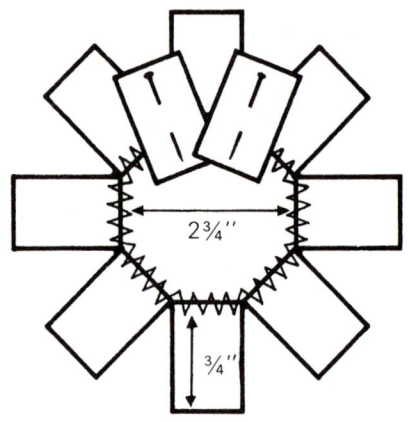

5, 6 Baby's angel top

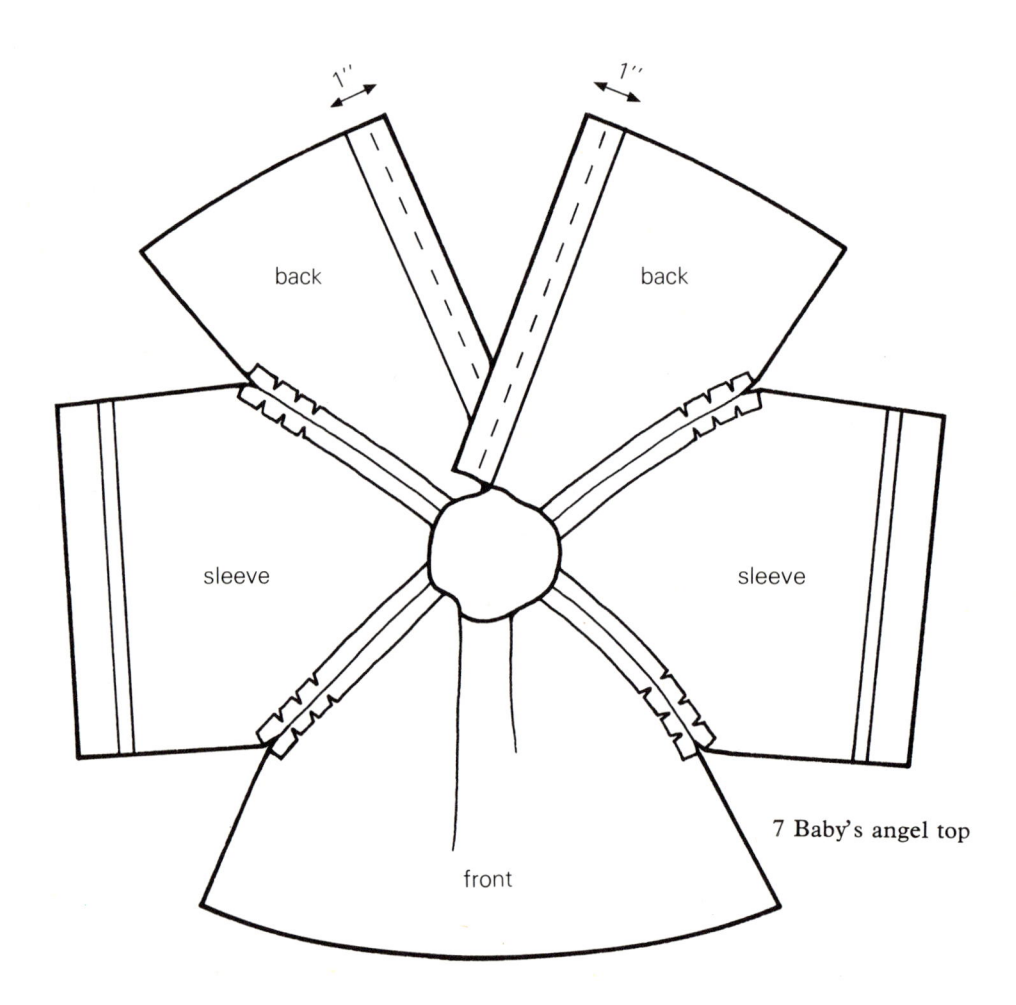

7 Baby's angel top

Baby's angel top

8 Make two rows of small running stitch around the top of the garment, and gather the neck to reduce the size of the opening to $11\frac{1}{2}''$.

9 Cut a piece of $\frac{7}{8}''$ wide pink ribbon $12\frac{1}{2}''$ long and pin it onto the right side of the neck edge allowing a $\frac{1}{2}''$ overlap at either end. Tack and sew the ribbon in place. Trim the neck edge and remove the gathering stitches. Fold the ribbon over in half, and sew it to the inside of the neck with tiny hemming stitches, thus enclosing all raw edges. Tuck the $\frac{1}{2}''$ overlaps inside the ribbon and oversew the ends.

10 Cut two pieces of narrow elastic 7" long. Using a large-eyed blunt needle, thread one through each strip of bias binding on the sleeves, and stitch into place at either end.

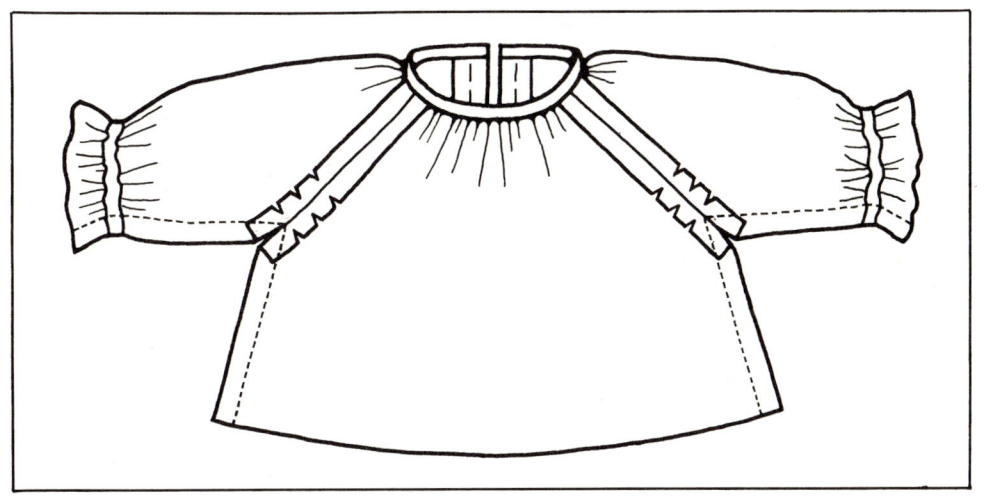

11 Baby's angel top: sewing the side and underarm seams

11 With right sides together, pin, tack, and stitch the side and underarm seams as one. Finish the bottom of the garment and the sleeves with $\frac{7}{8}''$ wide pink ribbon folded in half, and pin to enclose the raw edges. Tack and sew in place.

12 Make three buttonholes on one back piece and sew three buttons onto the other back piece. Finally sew a snap fastener (snapper or popper) at the neck edge. Alternatively, snap fasteners could be used instead of buttons.

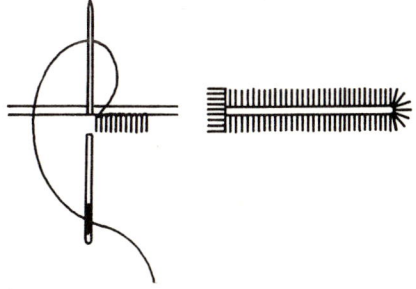

11 Baby's angel top: adding the pink trimming

12 Baby's angel top: making a buttonhole

Woven cushion

The amount of ribbon required obviously depends on the size of the cushion and the desired colour combinations. The texture should be kept constant, that is, velvet, satin, or rayon etc., although the width can be varied. Narrow ribbons produce the best woven results as broader ones are liable to slip, but for ribbon wider than $\frac{1}{2}''$, velvet is ideal, as the warp (lengthwise) and weft (cross) threads tend to cling together. A ready-made foam cushion could be used but, equally well, one can be made very simply. The measurements given here will make a cushion cover 18" by $12\frac{1}{2}''$, with woven ribbons both sides.

Materials
Filled cushion, or $\frac{1}{2}$ yard strong cotton or fine canvas 36" wide and $\frac{3}{4}$ lb kapok
$\frac{3}{4}$ yard cotton lining material 36" wide
Large rectangle of strong cardboard 18" by 13"
16 yards pink rayon or nylon ribbon $\frac{3}{8}''$ wide
18 yards orange rayon or nylon ribbon $\frac{3}{8}''$ wide
22 yards lilac rayon or nylon ribbon $\frac{3}{8}''$ wide
Weaving needle with a large eye
2 yards lilac satin ribbon 3" wide

The cushion
From the wide strong cotton material or fine canvas, cut out a piece 36" by $12\frac{1}{2}''$. With right sides together, fold it in half and machine stitch along the two sides, allowing a $\frac{1}{2}''$ seam. Leave the remaining end open so that when turned the right way out the cushion can be filled with kapok, foam chippings, or feathers. When this is done, turn in the raw edges $\frac{1}{2}''$ and machine stitch or oversew (overcast).

The cushion cover
1 Cut two pieces of cotton lining material several inches larger than the size of the finished cushion, in other words about 21" by 16".

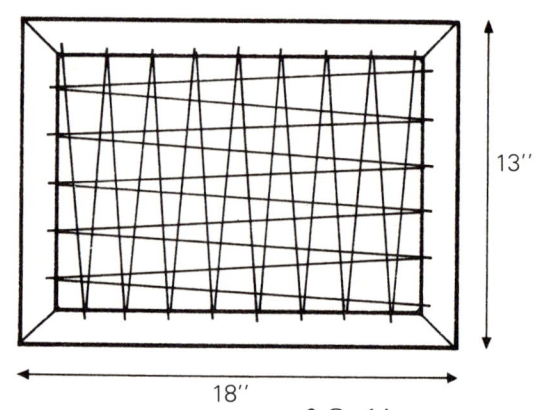

2 Cushion cover

2 Take one of these lining pieces and with the right side up, stretch it firmly (but not too tightly) and evenly over a large rectangular piece of strong cardboard 18" by 13". Secure on the reverse side of the card with large zigzag stitches $\frac{1}{2}''$ in from the edge.

3 Measure and cut 28 warp or lengthwise ribbons $16\frac{1}{2}''$ long. These can be arranged as illustrated, in which case cut 6 pink, 9 orange, and 13 lilac, or they can be arranged freely in any colour combination. Place a warp ribbon just to one side of the centre of the cardboard-backed lining material and secure it with a few small stitches about $\frac{1}{4}''$ in from each end.

4 Lay and secure another ribbon on the lining material, parallel to the first and just touching it. Continue laying warp ribbons in this way on either side of the centre ribbon.

Woven cushion

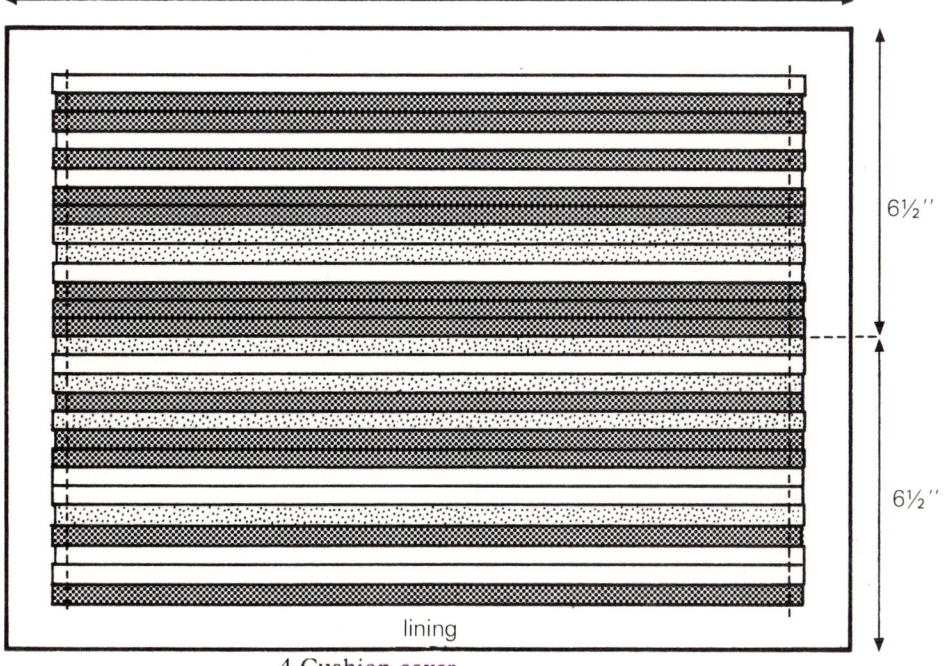

4 Cushion cover

5 Measure and cut 43 weft or cross ribbons 11" long (14 pink, 13 orange, 16 lilac). Thread one through the large-eyed needle and, starting at one end, weave it under and over the warp threads. Ease the weft ribbon up against the line of stitches holding the warp threads in place and again secure with small running stitches about $\frac{1}{4}"$ in from each end.

6 Thread the second weft ribbon and weave it through the warp threads, alternating with the previous weft ribbon so that where the first ribbon went under a warp thread the second goes over it. Continue in this way until all the weft ribbons have been woven.

7 Remove the zigzag securing stitches from the back and take out the cardboard. Machine over the running stitches around the edge of the woven ribbons. Cut away any surplus backing material, leaving about $\frac{1}{4}"$ extending beyond the ribbon ends.

6 Cushion cover

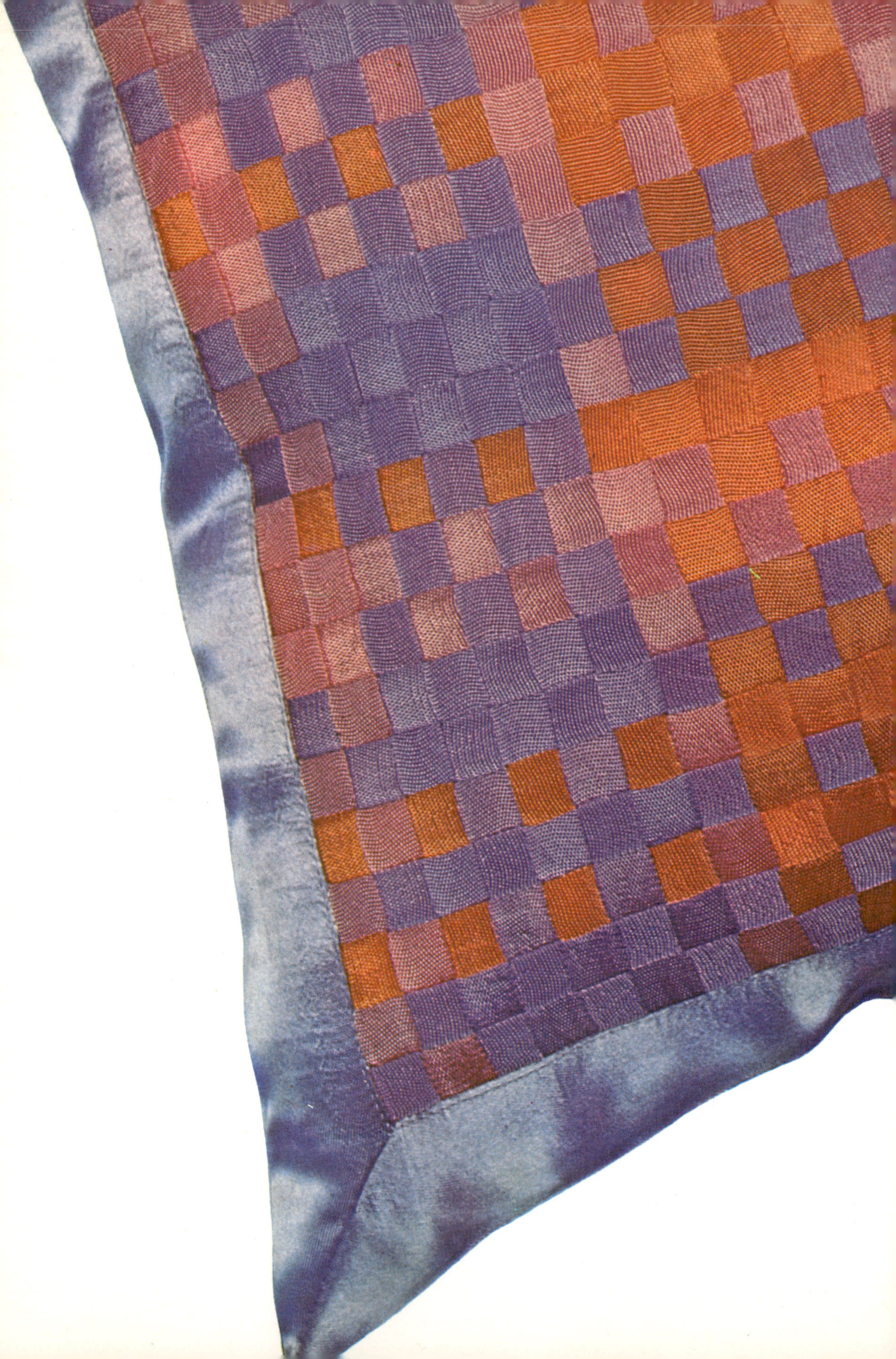

9 Cushion cover: mitering the corners

8   Repeat instructions 2 to 7 for the back of the cushion cover.

9   Carefully measure the lilac satin ribbon round the edge of the cover, such that it overlaps the raw ends and one row of woven ribbons. Mark the corners and fold them over with right sides facing. Mitre each corner with diagonal lines of stitches as shown, and join the ends at a corner. Turn the ribbon the right way out, fold along its centre, and press.

Dried flowers

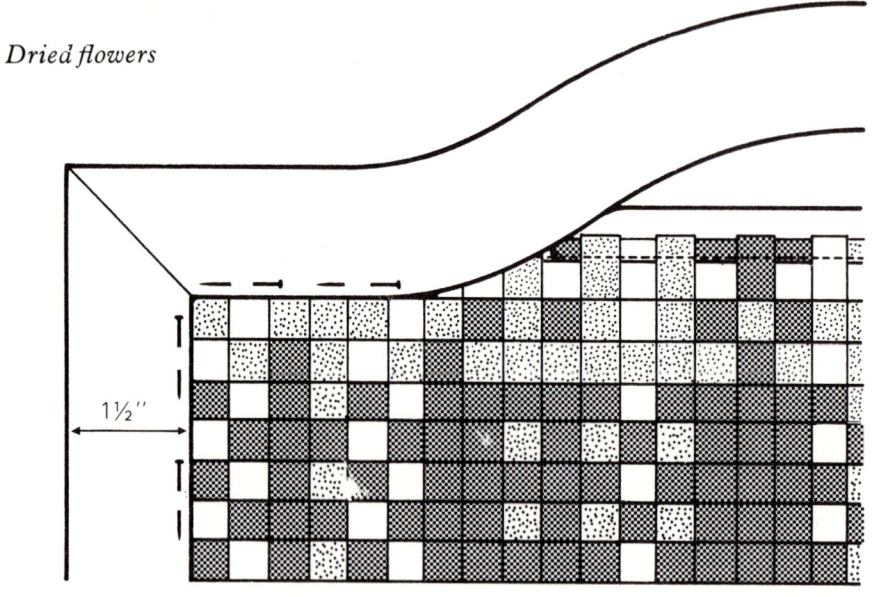

1½"

10 Cushion cover

10 Pin 3" wide lilac ribbon around the four edges of one of the woven pieces and tack and machine in place with the overlap indicated above. Repeat this for the other woven piece, but leave one narrow side open. Press the cushion cover. Insert the filled cushion and carefully oversew (overcast) the remaining seam.

Dried flowers

Ribbons combine very naturally with dried flowers when making sprays, lavender bags, and pomanders, and they can be used lavishly with plenty of frills and bows.

Lavender spray

Materials
Bunch of dried lavender
½ yard cream ribbon ¼" wide
1½ yards yellow ribbon ¼" wide

1 Cut the stalks of the lavender to equal lengths (about 6") and divide the bunch equally into two. Place the tips of the stalks of one bunch at the base of the flower heads of the other, and bind the stalks together tightly with cotton.

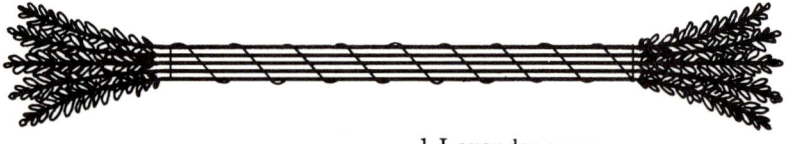

1 Lavender spray

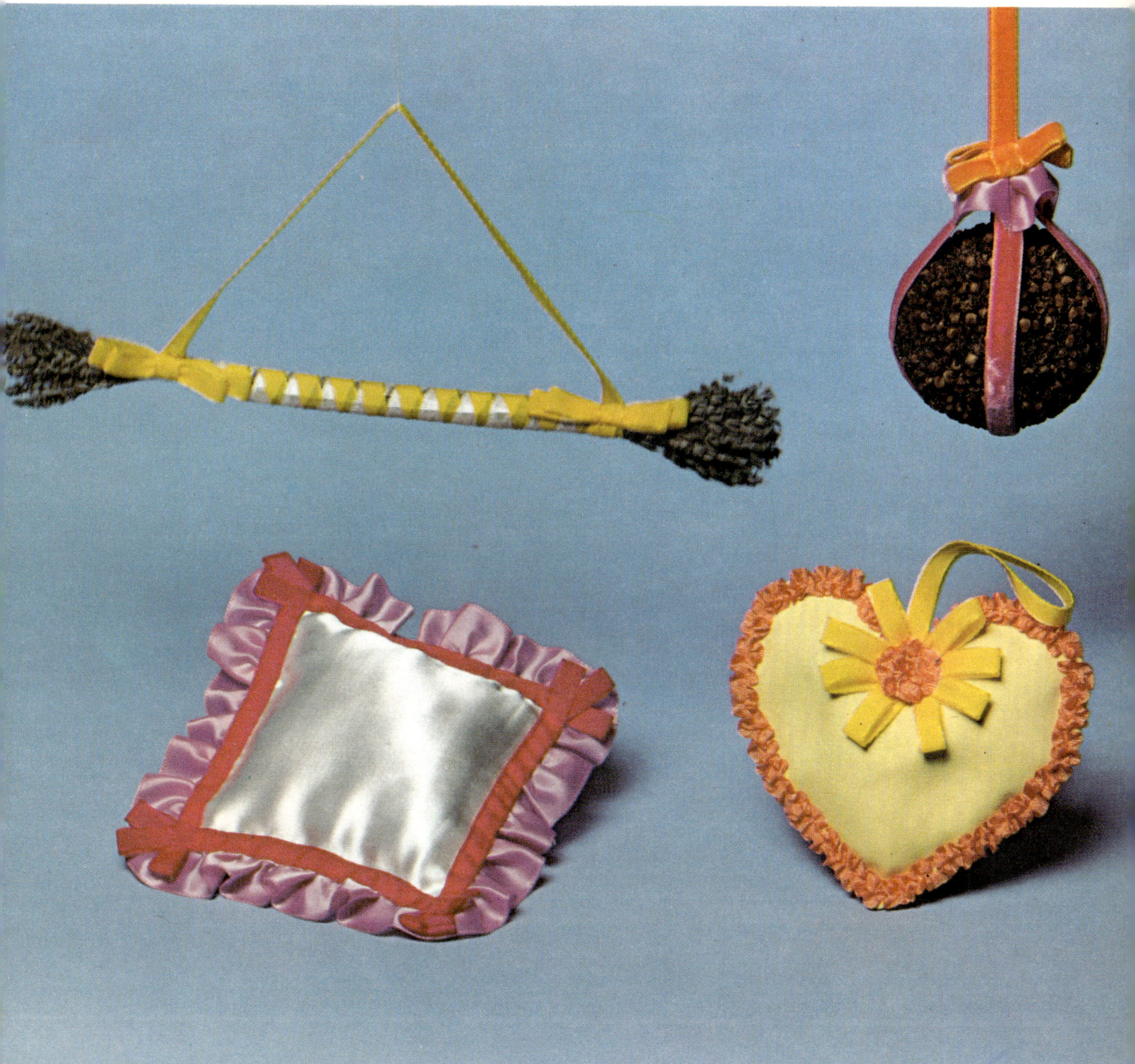

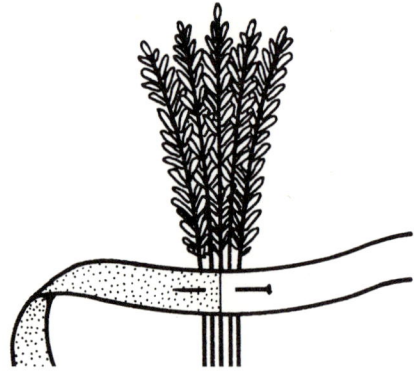

Dried flowers

2 Lavender spray

2 Take two 18" pieces of ribbon, one cream and one yellow, and stitch one raw end of each together. Pin this join, with the seam on the inside, onto the lavender stalks just below the flower heads.

3 On the opposite side of the stalks to the pin, cross the cream ribbon diagonally over the yellow one. Turn the spray over again and this time cross the yellow ribbon over the cream one. Continue weaving the ribbons in this way, making the diagonals tight enough so that the stalks are covered. Stitch the ribbons in place at both ends of the spray.

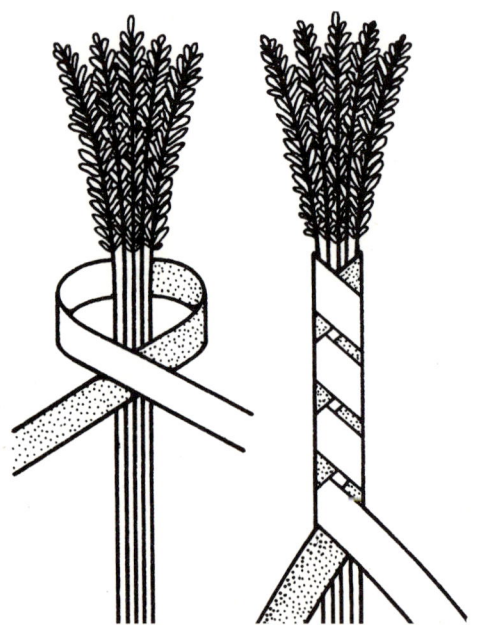

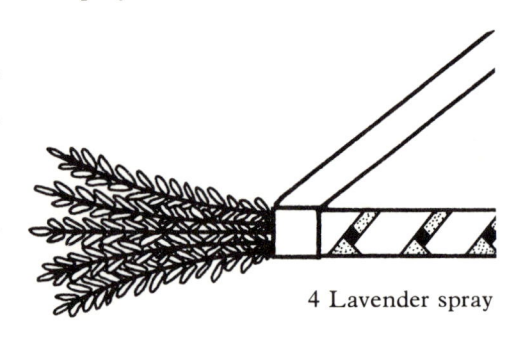

3 Lavender spray

4 Lavender spray

4 Cut a piece of yellow ribbon 12" long for the hanger. Bind this ribbon over the ends of the woven ribbon at each end just below the flower heads and secure with a few tiny stitches.

5 Make two double bows from 7" lengths of yellow ribbon folded as shown, and secure with a few stitches at the centre. Cover these securing stitches with a $\frac{3}{4}"$ length of yellow ribbon sewn at the back. Attach one of these bows at each end of the ribbon hanger.

5 Lavender spray

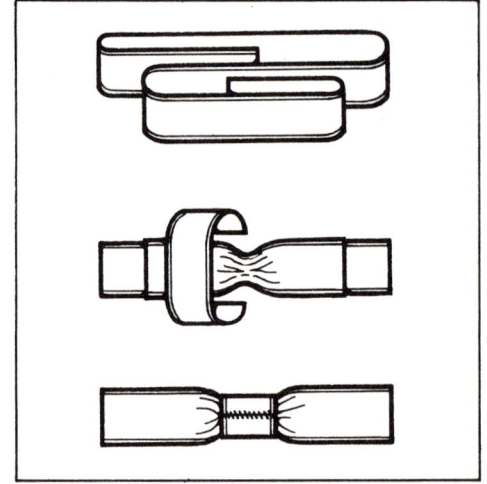

Dried flowers

Square lavender bag

Materials
1 yard pink ribbon $\frac{3}{4}''$ wide
$\frac{1}{4}$ yard white satin ribbon 4" wide
1 yard dark pink ribbon $\frac{1}{4}''$ wide
Dried lavender flowers

1 Cut a piece of $\frac{3}{4}''$ wide pink ribbon 33" long, fold it in half, and join the ends with a $\frac{1}{2}''$ seam to form a circle. Trim one end of the seam and fold the other end over it, turning the ribbon under $\frac{1}{4}''$, so that all the raw ends are covered. Place four marker pins 8" apart around the ribbon. Along one edge make two rows of running stitch close together and gather this edge to just under half its original length.

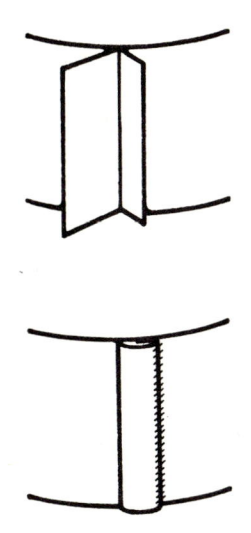

1 Square lavender bag: covering the raw ends of the seam

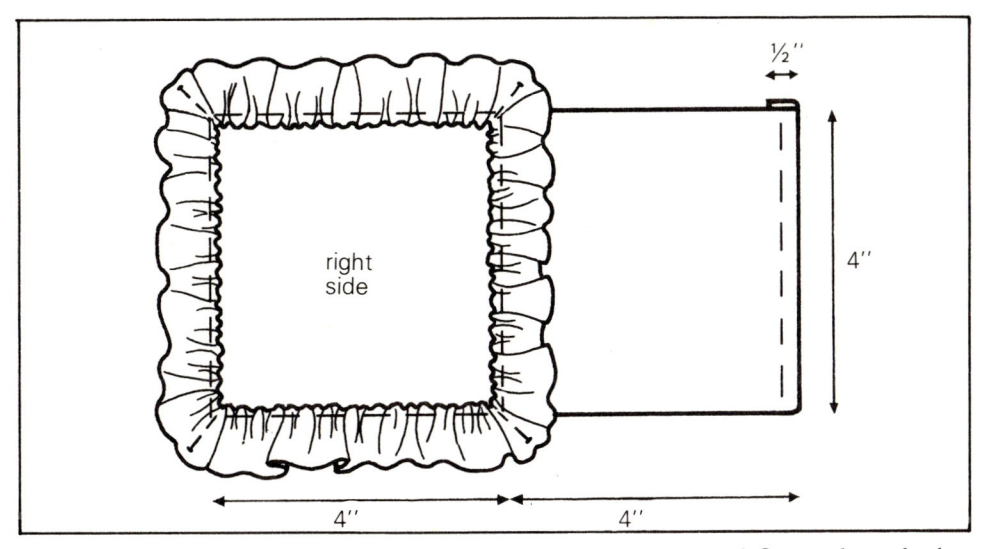

3 Square lavender bag

2 Tack the raw ends of a 9" piece of white satin ribbon under $\frac{1}{2}''$. Mark the centre line (parallel with the raw ends) with a row of tacking stitch.

3 With the right side of the white ribbon uppermost, pin the gathered pink ribbon exactly over the left half of the white ribbon so that the marker pins are at each corner. Tack the gathered ribbon onto the white base.

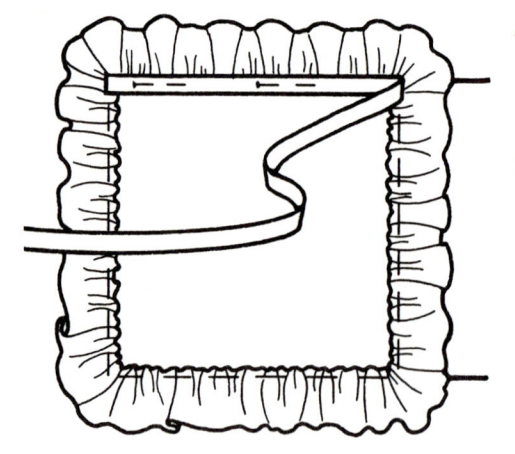

Dried flowers

4 Square lavender bag

4 Starting at one corner, pin dark ribbon over one of the gathered edges of the lighter pink ribbon, but within the 4" square of white ribbon.

5 At the corner of the bag, extend the dark pink ribbon to the outer edge of the gathered ribbon. Turn it back on itself and then make two more folds, one at 45° and one at right angles. Follow the diagrams carefully. Continue pinning the dark pink ribbon around the bag, making identical folds in each corner. Overlap the starting point $\frac{1}{2}$" and turn the trimmed ribbon end under $\frac{1}{4}$".

5 Square lavender bag

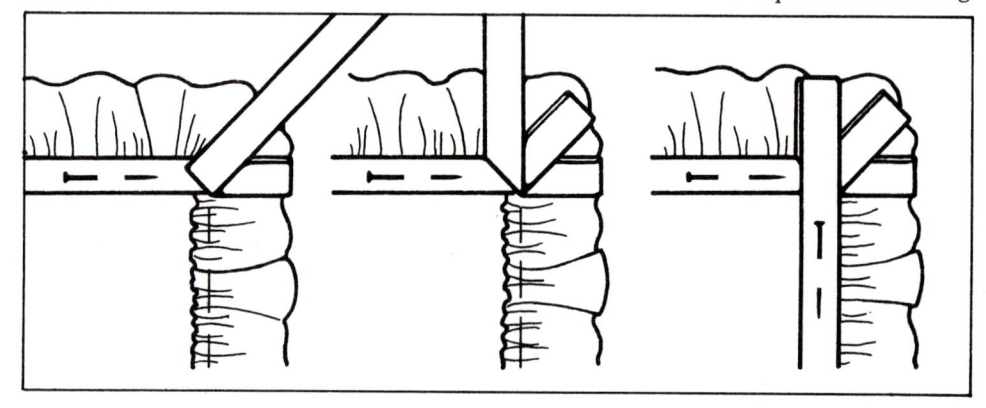

6 Tack and sew around both edges of the dark pink ribbon. This stitching will hold the two pink decorating ribbons in place on the white square.

7 On the reverse side of the bag fold the other half of the white ribbon back over the first half and stitch it in place along the two sides close to the edge.

8 Fill with dried lavender flowers and oversew (overcast) the remaining edge.

8 Square lavender bag

Dried flowers

Heart-shaped lavender bag

Materials
Sheet of tracing paper
2 pieces of yellow cotton material each 6" square
1½ yards orange ribbon ¼" wide
1¼ yards yellow ribbon ¼" wide
Strip of cardboard 2¼" wide

1 Make a paper pattern in the dimensions shown and cut out two heart shapes from two 6" squares of yellow cotton material. With the right sides of the material together, join the two pieces, allowing a ¼" seam and leaving a small opening about 1½" wide on one of the long sides.

1 Heart-shaped lavender bag

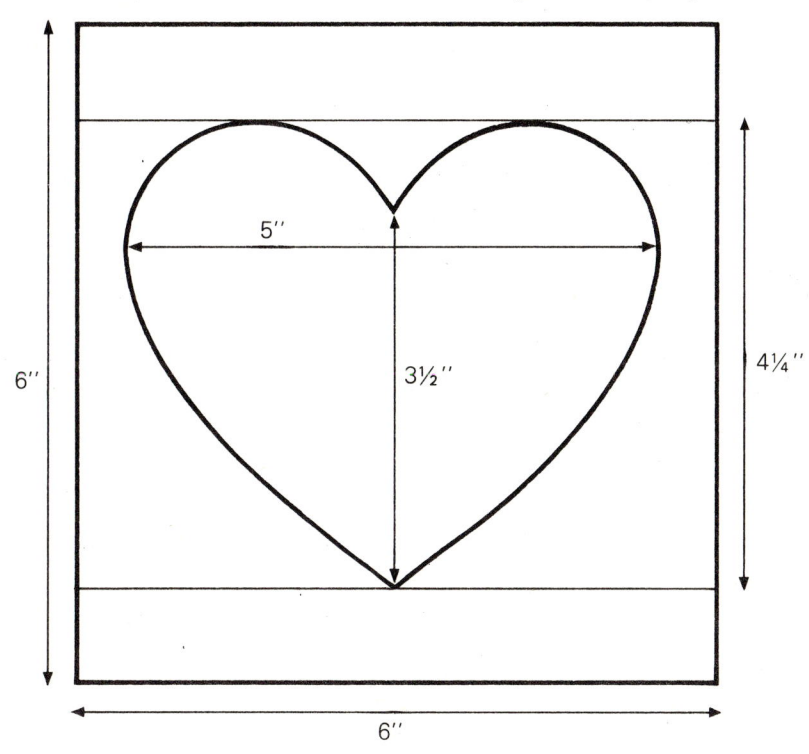

2 Heart-shaped lavender bag

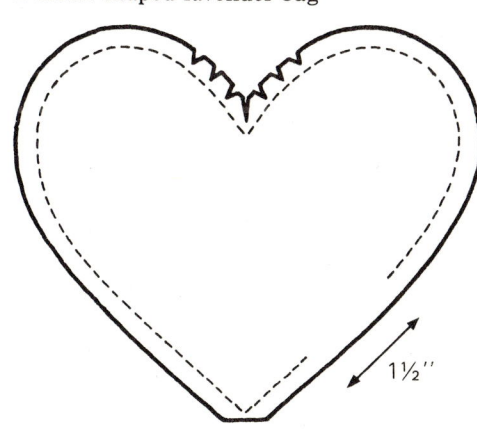

2 Make tiny cuts into the seam at the top and cut away the point at the tip of the heart.

3 Turn the bag the right way out, press it, and then pack it loosely with dried lavender flowers. Oversew (overcast) the opening.

Dried flowers

4 Heart-shaped lavender bag

4 Gather 42" of narrow orange ribbon with a central line of running stitch and pin this gathered ribbon round the edge of the bag. Sew it in place by hand with back stitch along its centre and then remove the gathering stitches.

5 Make a loop from a 7" piece of yellow ribbon and stitch it to the centre top of the heart at the base of the frill to form a hanger.

6 Wind a length of yellow ribbon four times round a piece of cardboard $2\frac{1}{4}"$ wide, leaving a small overlap. Slip the ribbon off the card and, holding it flat, make two very small cuts on either side of the ribbon at the centre.

6 Heart-shaped lavender bag

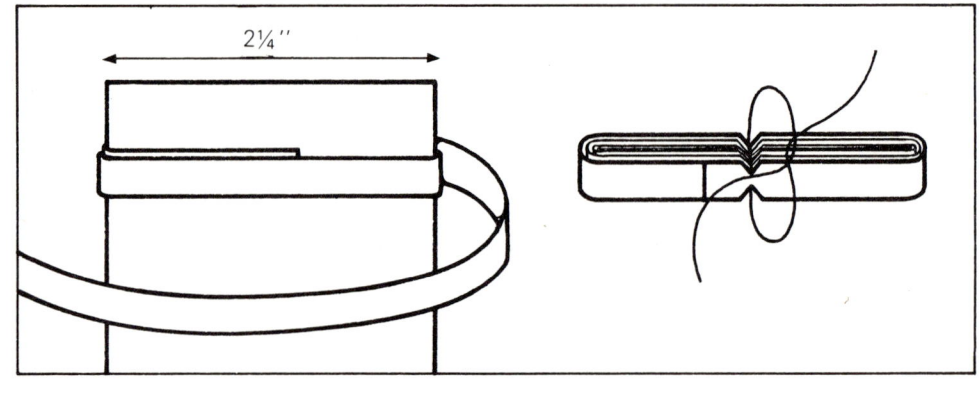

7 Tie a piece of cotton round the middle of the folded ribbon at the cuts, and fan out the separate loops to form a star shape. Stitch this onto the heart at the base of the looped hanger.

8 Gather the remaining orange ribbon tightly to make a rosette and stitch it at the centre of the yellow ribbon star.

7 Heart-shaped lavender bag

Dried flowers

Pomander

Materials
1 small orange
2 to 3 oz dried cloves
1 oz powdered cinnamon
1 oz powdered orris root
Sheet of tissue paper
½ yard orange velvet ribbon ¼" wide
½ yard dark pink velvet ribbon ¼" wide
¼ yard pink satin ribbon ⅞" wide

1   Take a small orange and press dried cloves into it, either covering it completely or leaving two bands free of cloves to take a ribbon. These bands should not be covered yet as the orange will shrink on drying out.

2   Put one tablespoon of a powder made from equal parts of powdered cinnamon and powdered orris root into a small polythene bag, add the orange, and coat it with the powder so that it becomes well impregnated. Remove the orange from the bag, wrap it in tissue paper and leave it to dry in a warm place for about two weeks.

3   Encircle the orange with two loops of dark pink velvet ribbon and sew tightly. Stitch on a 7" loop of orange velvet ribbon for a hanger at the top of the orange where the encircling pink ribbons cross.

4   Over the hanger loop, slip a rosette made from a 7" strip of pink satin ribbon gathered along one edge. Stitch in place at the bottom of the loop.

5   Add two tiny orange velvet bows made from 3" lengths of ribbon and stitch these to either side of the hanger loop.

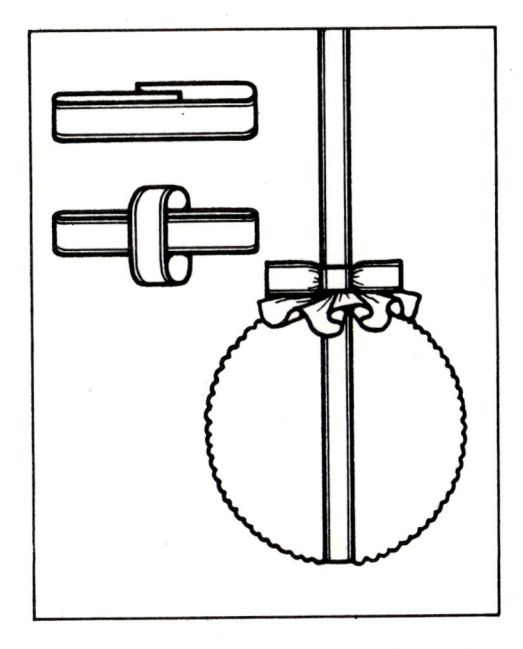

1 Pomander

5 Pomander

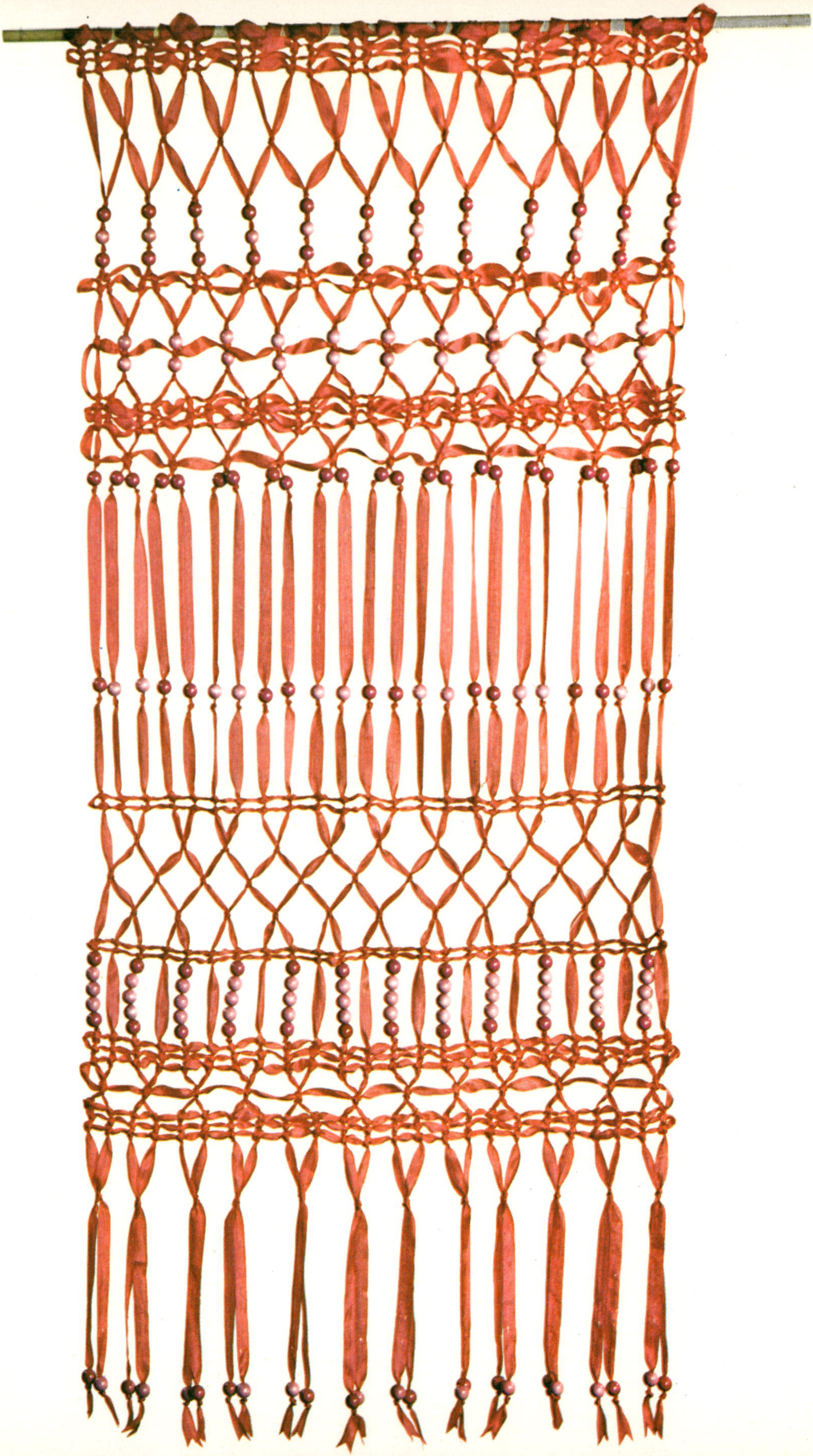

Macramé hanging

Theoretically ribbon is not the most suitable material for macramé as this form of knotting is based on rounded not flat threads, but in practice ribbons knotted together produce a pretty, lacy effect. The piece illustrated was designed to hang in a small window, so the ribbons have been widely spaced to allow light to pass through. However it could be made on a much larger scale as a room divider, in which case more and wider ribbons should be used. The amount of ribbon needed varies considerably according to the structure of the work. Obviously a piece composed of closely mounted ribbons and many knots will require more than did the illustrated design. In this instance the ribbons, which were mounted double, were originally one and a half times the length of the finished work (36 yards were needed), and 27 yards of ribbon were needed for the horizontal rows of knotting. This made a hanging 15″ wide and 34″ long. Macramé is based on three basic knots but only two of these, the overhand and the double half hitch, were used to form this hanging. Beads were also incorporated into the design. The only extra equipment required is a large, flat, foam rubber cushion, which makes an excellent knotting surface—the ribbons are held in place on the cushion with pins. The macramé can be moved up the cushion as the work progresses, but larger designs are best worked as they hang, on a wall.

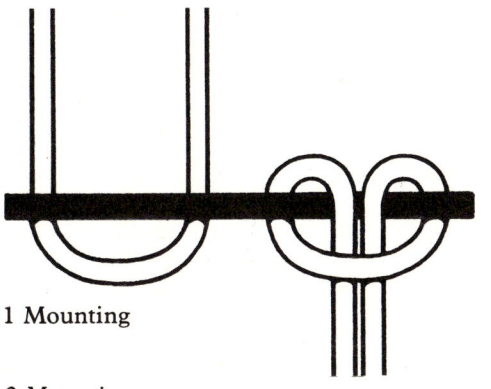

Materials
63 yards pink ribbon $\frac{1}{4}$″ wide
20″ long wooden rod (about $\frac{3}{8}$″ diameter)
96 mauve beads
94 pink beads

Mounting
1   Cut twelve 3 yard pieces of ribbon. Fold one of the pieces in half with the loop pointing away, and place the wooden rod on top. Bring the loop over the rod, pass the two free ends through, and draw up tightly, pulling the ends downwards.

2   Take the left-hand free end of ribbon above the rod and make a loop, holding it in place with a pin. Using the same piece of ribbon make a double half hitch as shown.

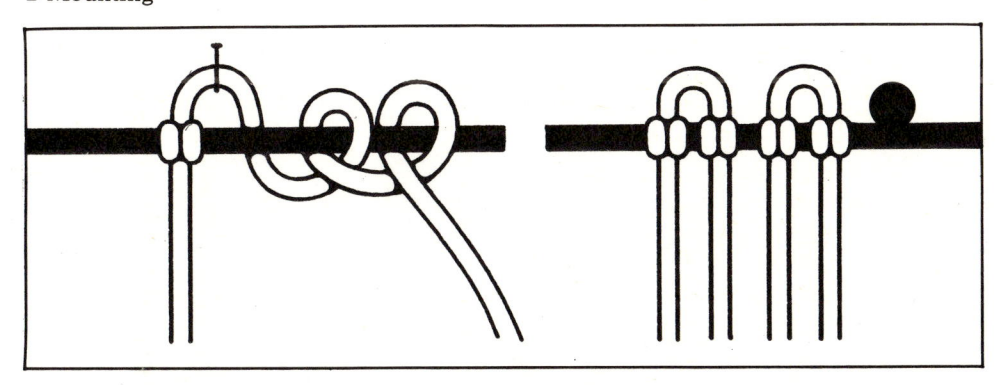

1 Mounting

2 Mounting

Macramé hanging

3 Mount all twelve ribbons in this way and space them regularly. Alternatively the ribbons can be mounted simply without the extra loop and the double half hitch.

4 Using any combination of the knots described below, the macramé is now ready to be made. Beads can be worked into the design to add interest—in fact, their weight helps to keep the ribbons hanging straight.

The overhand knot
This simple knot is tied with one length of ribbon and is used in combination with other ribbons to make the diamond shapes or netting pattern, and also to hold the beads in place. The end of the ribbon is taken up, round, and through the loop it has made.

Overhand knot

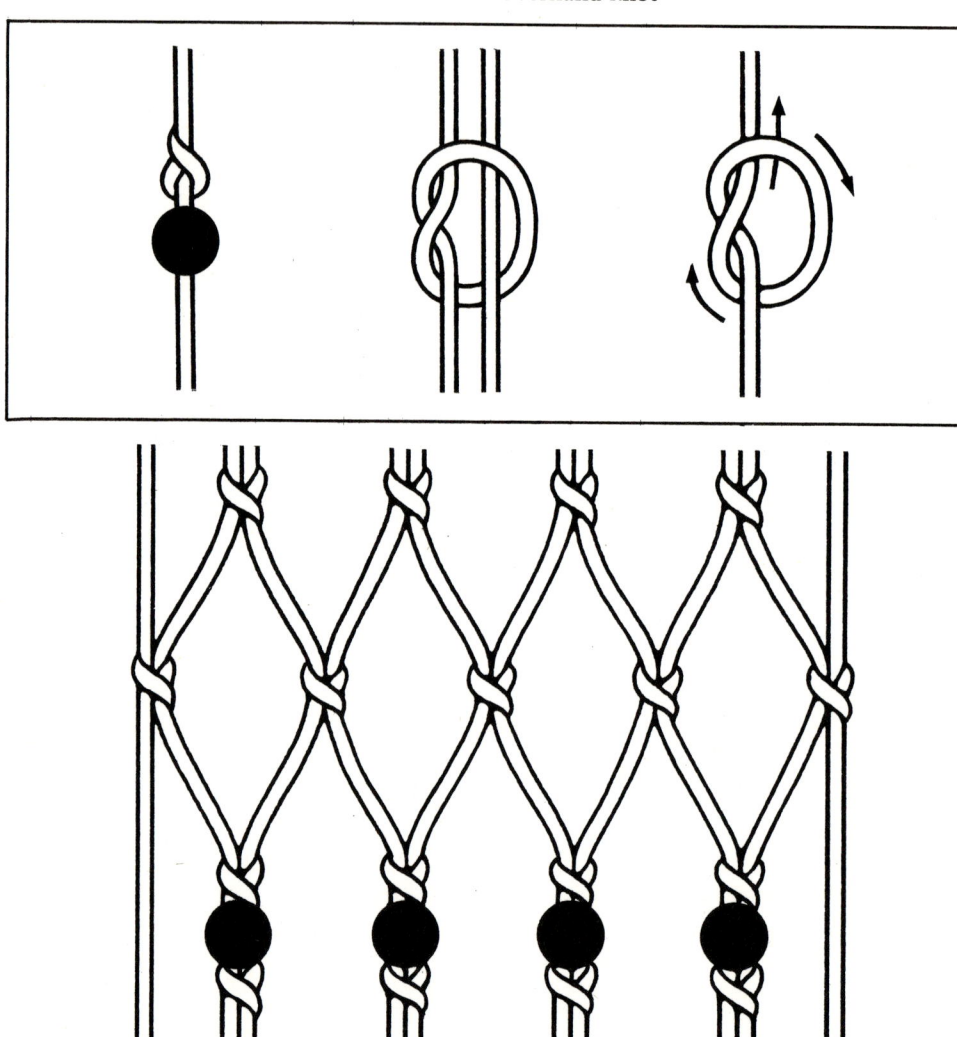

Overhand knot: making diamond shapes

Macramé hanging

The double half hitch
This knot is tied with two lengths of ribbon, one being the carrying ribbon and the other the knotting ribbon. The carrying ribbon, which holds the knots, is always placed over the knotting ribbon and determines the direction of a row. The knots can be made horizontally or vertically, but in either case horizontal ribbons (of varying lengths) are needed to work with the vertical ones. Before starting, the ends of the horizontal ribbons are knotted, and they are held in place with pins while working.

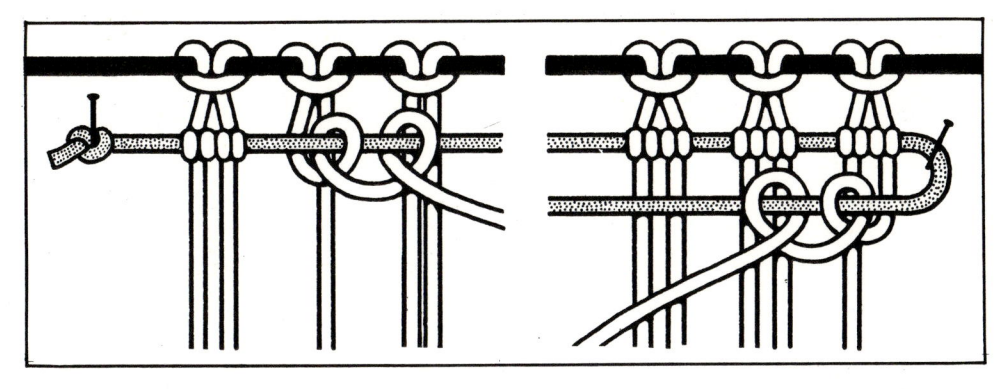

1 Place the carrying ribbon over the knotting ribbon and loop the knotting ribbon twice round the carrying ribbon and draw up tightly as shown. This applies to horizontal and vertical knotting.

1 Double half hitch: horizontal knotting

2 Double half hitch: vertical knotting

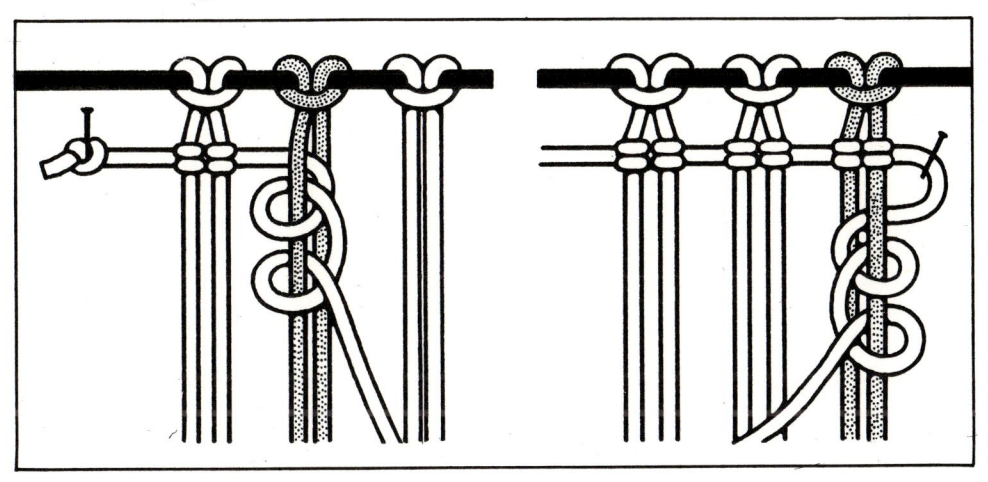

2 When a required number of rows of double half hitches have been worked, cut the knotting ribbon (which could be either a vertical or a horizontal piece of ribbon) close to the edge of the work and stitch the raw edge in place on the reverse side of the macramé to prevent fraying. Alternatively, the knotting ribbon can be left trailing to form part of the pattern. This instruction also applies to the start of the horizontal ribbons.

Patchwork cover

To make a piece of patchwork use ribbons and braids of as many different widths and patterns as possible. The weight of the ribbons should be similar, for example do not use velvet with nylon ribbon as the former is too bulky. Ribbon patchwork has an advantage over other kinds in that the pieces have two woven edges which will not fray. This cover could be used for photograph albums, stamp books, scrap books etc., and the illustrated one is approximately 8" by 12".

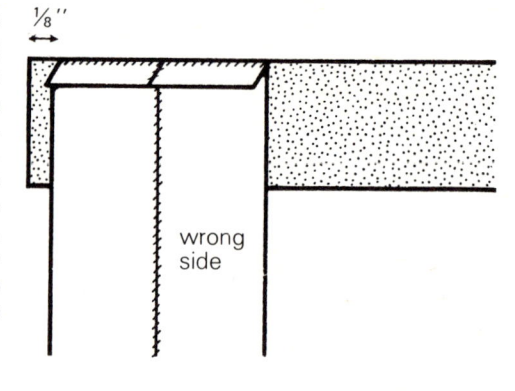

Materials
Odd pieces of ribbon and braid
Ribbon for edging 1" wide
Album or book with stiff cover
Rayon or nylon lining material

1   With right sides facing, oversew (overcast) any two, short, equal lengths of ribbon together to form a base for the patchwork. Unfold the two ribbons and lay flat.

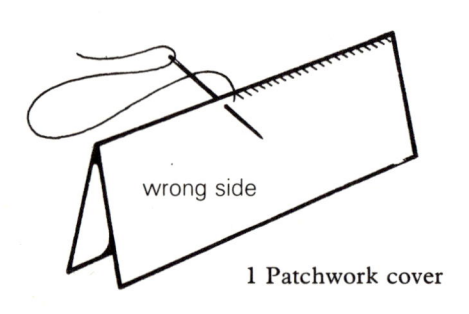

1 Patchwork cover

2 Patchwork cover

2   Turn one set of raw ends under $\frac{1}{8}"$, and with right sides together oversew (overcast) this folded edge to another contrasting ribbon, allowing the latter to overlap $\frac{1}{8}"$ at one end. Fold out the contrasting ribbon. Continue building in this way, using a variety of lengths and widths of ribbon, until a rectangular piece of patchwork large enough to cover the front and back panels and the spine of the album has been made. Always oversew (overcast) with right sides together, leave $\frac{1}{8}"$ overlap at raw ends for turning under, and fold flat the pieces each time.

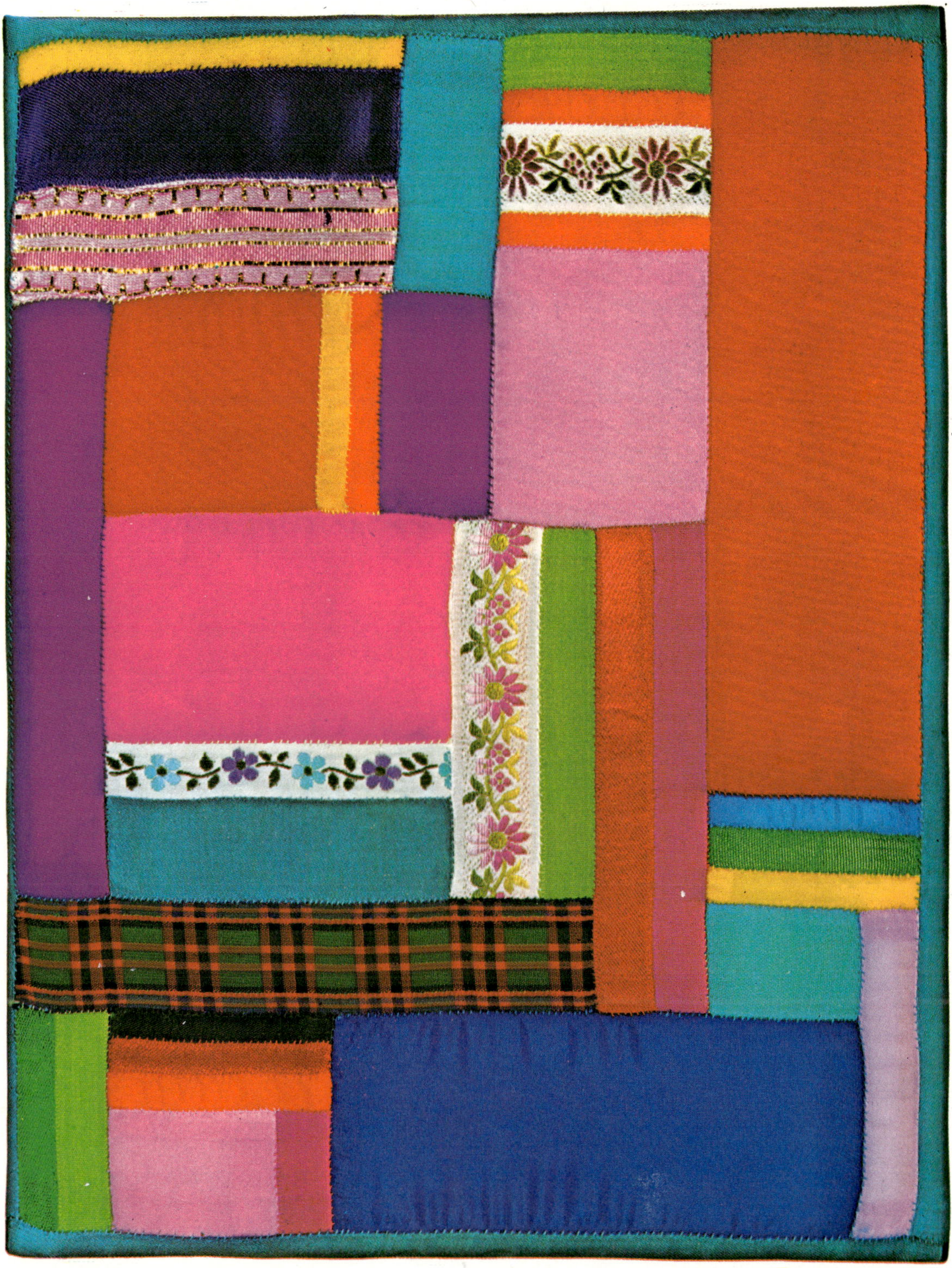

Patchwork cover

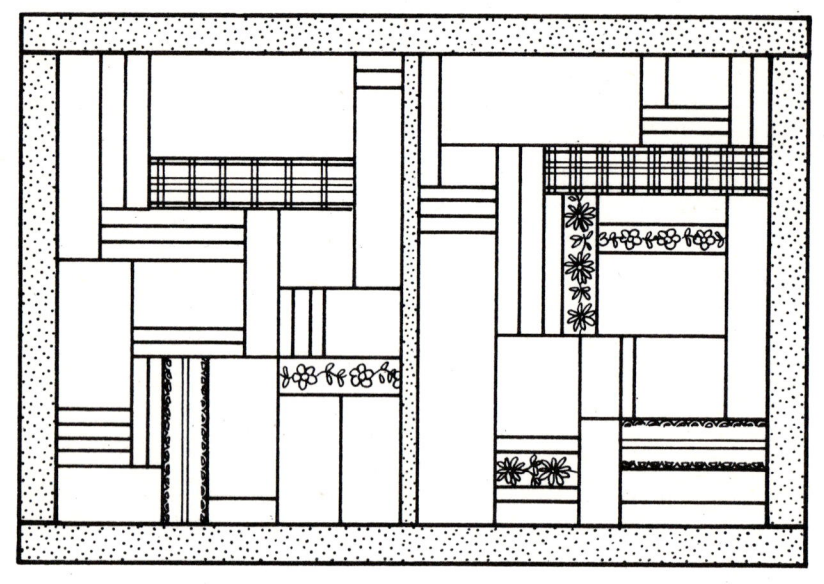

3 Patchwork cover

3 Again with right sides together, oversew (overcast) a piece of 1" wide ribbon down each side of the patchwork to form a neat edging. Then add two more pieces of the same 1" wide ribbon across the top and bottom of the work — the ribbon edging should extend beyond the album by about $\frac{3}{4}$" to $\frac{7}{8}$".

4 Press the patchwork to make it as flat as possible. Position it over the album and hold it in place at each corner with a pin. Gently stretch the patchwork over the cover, pinning it along the edges. Do not push the pins too far into the cover or they may damage it.

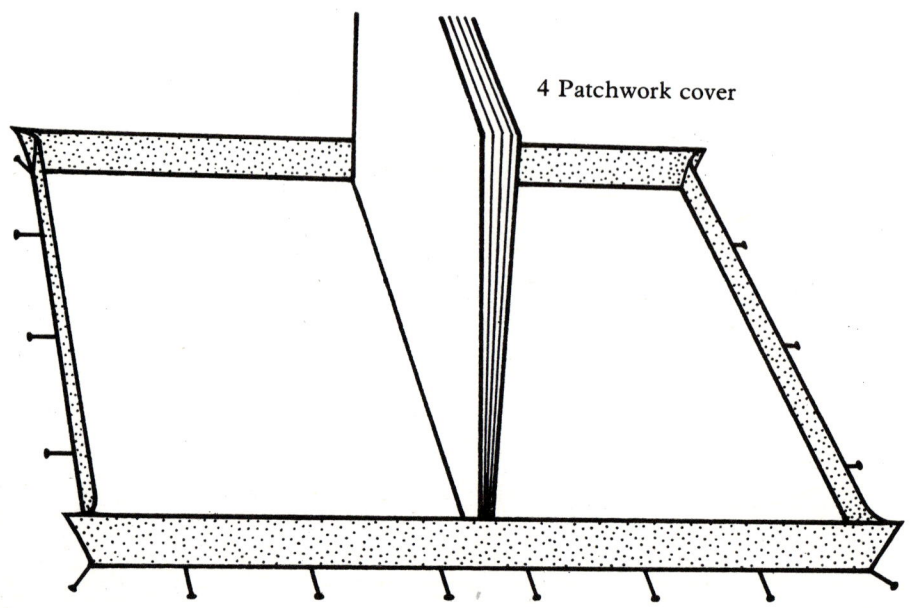

4 Patchwork cover

Patchwork cover

5 With the album open, make a cut into the edging ribbon either side of the spine (or a single cut at the spine if it is narrower than $\frac{1}{4}''$). Fold the edging ribbon over to the inside of the cover and mitre the corners, that is make diagonal folds, and sew in position.

6 Cut two identical pieces of lining material 1" wider and 1" longer than each half of the cover and turn a $\frac{1}{2}''$ hem around both. Pin one piece over the edging ribbons on the inside of the front cover and one on the inside of the back cover. Oversew (overcast) the lining to the patchwork, removing the pins as the sewing progresses.

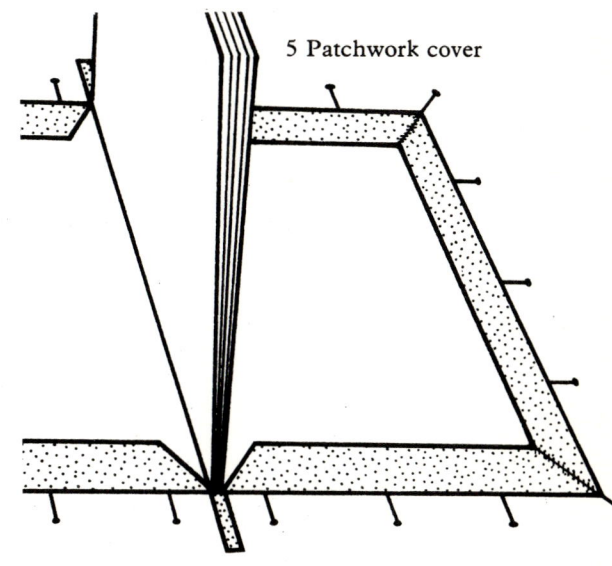

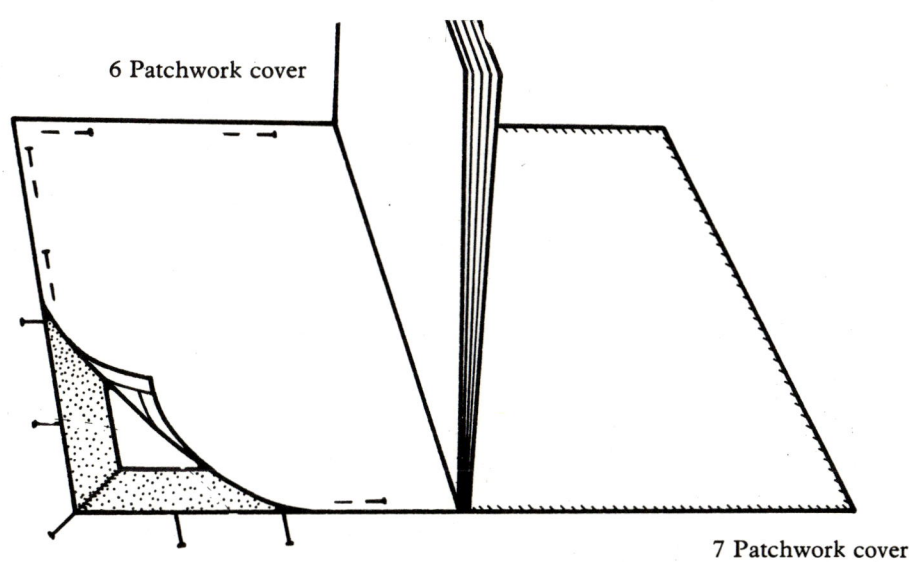

5 Patchwork cover

6 Patchwork cover

7 Patchwork cover

7 Fold the cover backwards and slip it off the album. Turn the small rectangles of ribbon remaining at the spine inwards and very carefully sew them to the spine with tiny stitches to prevent fraying.

8 Give the cover a final press with a cool iron and replace it on the album.

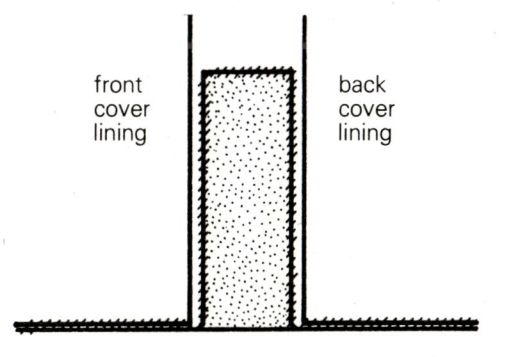

Shopping bag

This large shopping bag is decorated with cross stitch worked in ribbon on the front panel and along the handle. Any embroidery stitch can be worked in narrow ribbon but the background material must be loosely woven from thick fibres so that the spaces between the threads are large enough for the ribbon to pass through easily (otherwise, if the ribbon has to be forced through, it becomes damaged). Cross stitch is most easily worked on material with warp and weft threads of even thickness—the squares for each cross can then be simply measured by the number of threads.

Materials
¾ yard canvas or coarse fabric 45" wide for the bag (about 14 threads to one inch)
¾ yard strong cotton 36" wide for the lining
Strip of interfacing 28½" by 1¾"
37 yards mauve ribbon ¼" wide
15 yards yellow ribbon ¼" wide
13 yards olive ribbon ¼" wide
13 yards lilac ribbon ¼" wide
3 yards blue ribbon ¼" wide
3 yards orange ribbon ¼" wide

1 Cut a piece of canvas or coarse fabric 45" long and 16½" wide for the bag and a piece 28½" long and 5" wide for the handle. Also cut a piece of lining material (strong cotton is most suitable) 19" long and 31" wide, and a piece of interfacing for the handle 28½" long and 1¾" wide.

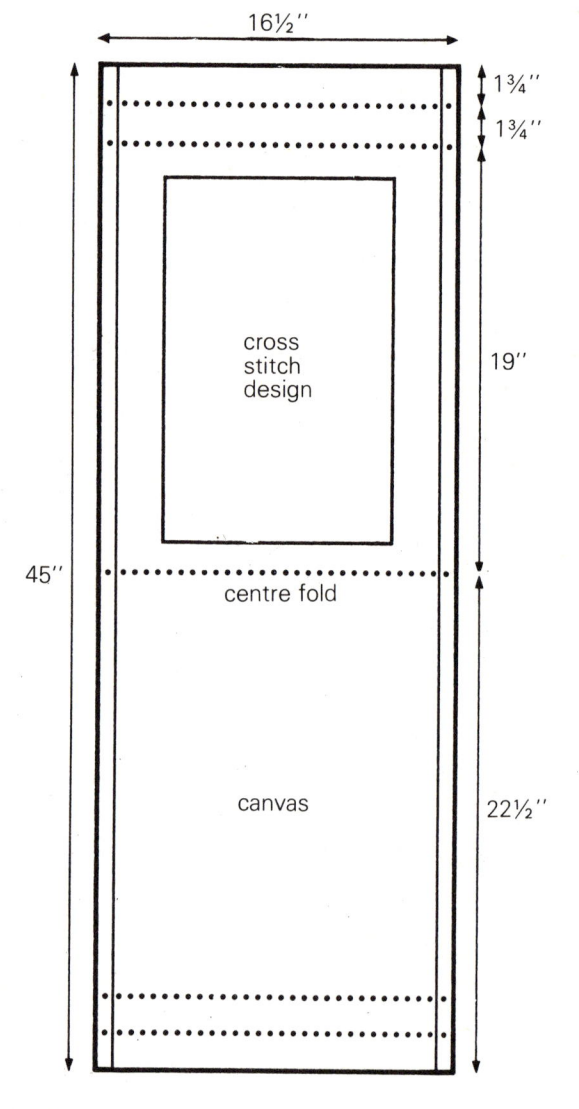

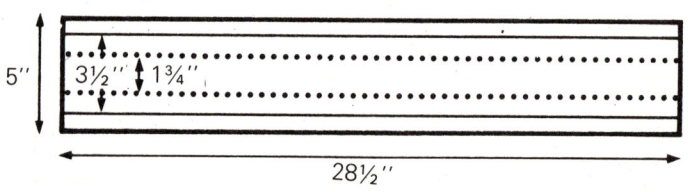

1 Shopping bag

Shopping bag

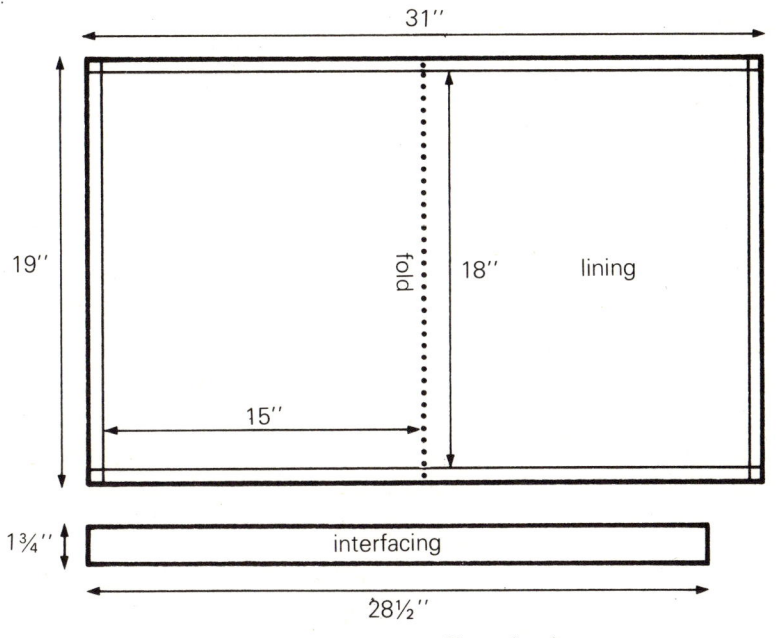

Shopping bag

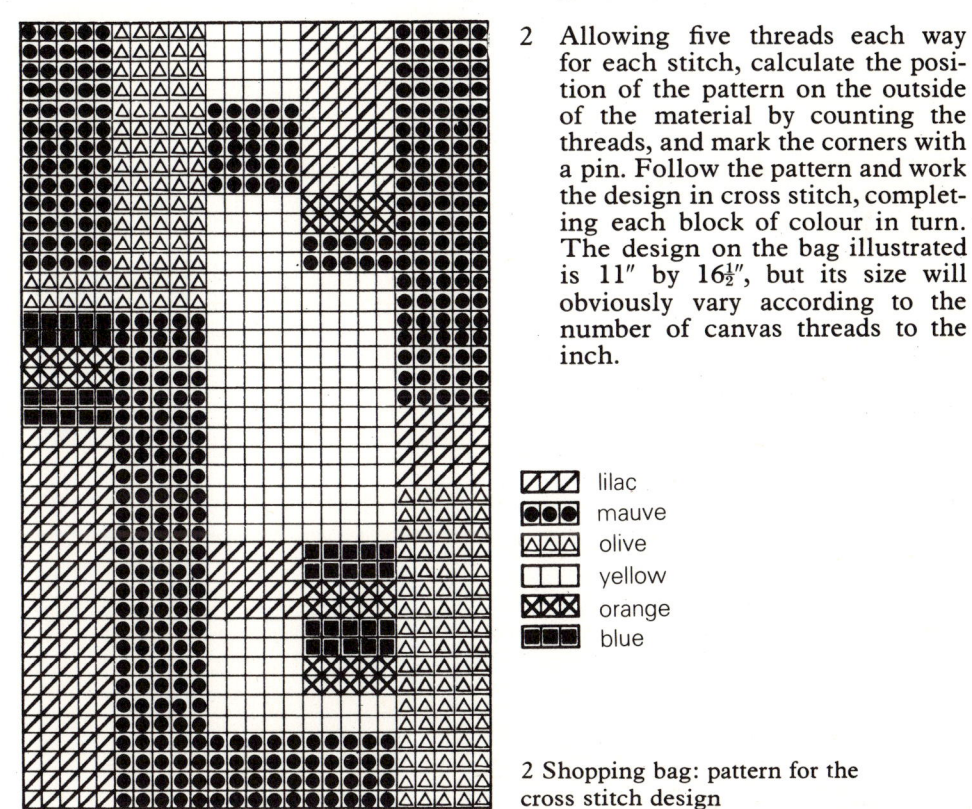

2 Allowing five threads each way for each stitch, calculate the position of the pattern on the outside of the material by counting the threads, and mark the corners with a pin. Follow the pattern and work the design in cross stitch, completing each block of colour in turn. The design on the bag illustrated is 11″ by $16\frac{1}{2}$″, but its size will obviously vary according to the number of canvas threads to the inch.

lilac
mauve
olive
yellow
orange
blue

2 Shopping bag: pattern for the cross stitch design

107

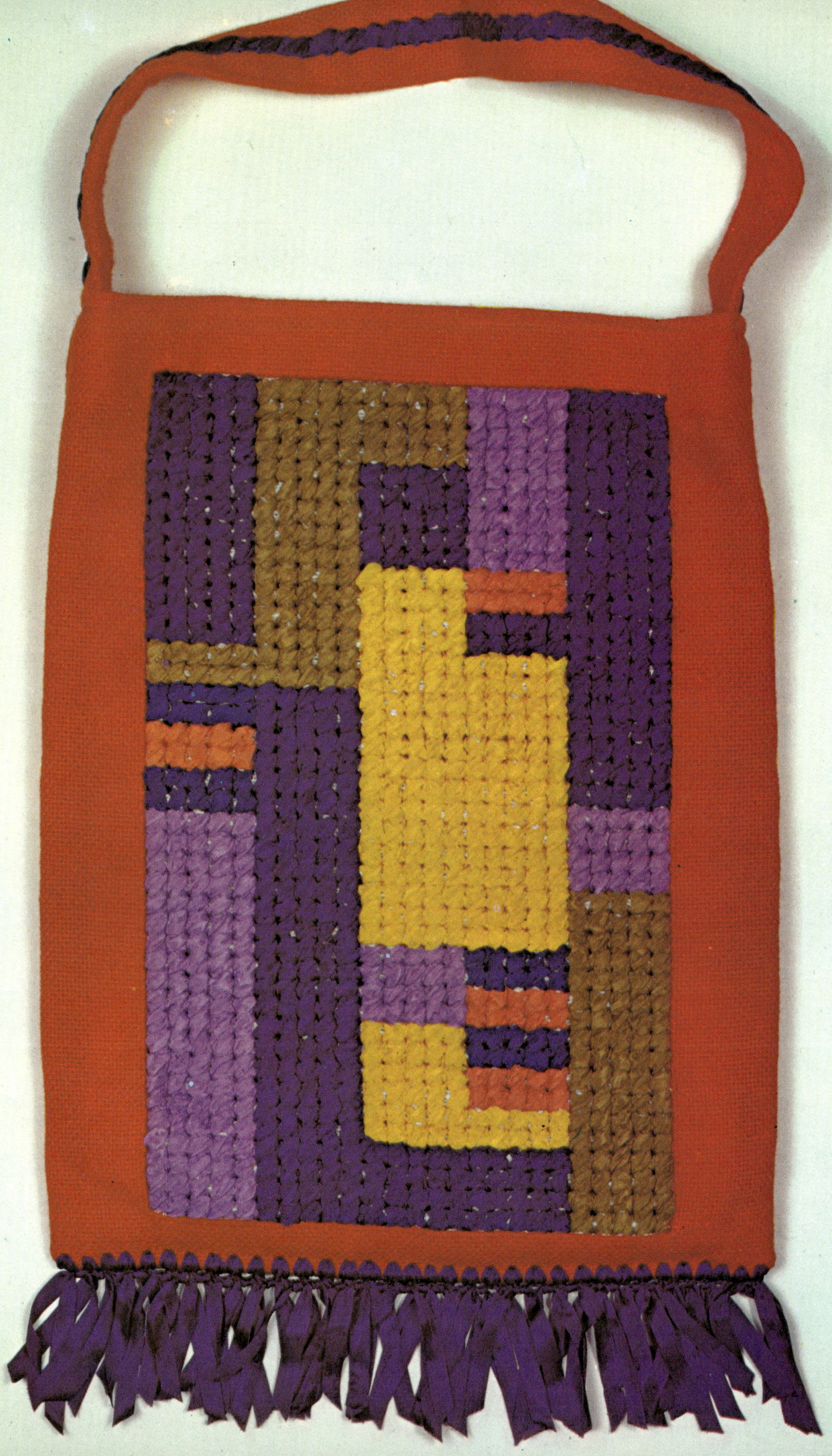

Shopping bag

3 Down the length and in the centre of the piece of material to be used as the handle, work one row of cross stitch in mauve ribbon.

4 Fold the bag in half with right sides together and sew $\frac{3}{4}''$ side seams. Oversew (overcast) the edges to prevent fraying, and fold them towards the back of the bag and press flat.

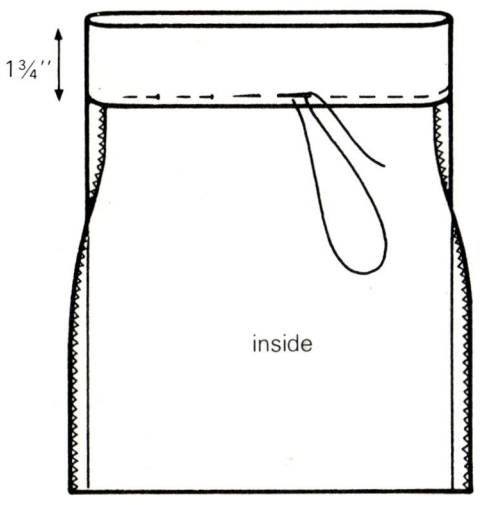

6 Shopping bag

5 Shopping bag

5 Keeping the bag inside out, fold the open end over $1\frac{3}{4}''$ and then over another $1\frac{3}{4}''$ to form a strong top for the bag and a strong base for the handle. Tack down the bottom edge of this hem. Machine stitch along the top of the bag $\frac{1}{4}''$ from the edge.

6 Place the piece of interfacing centrally along the handle on the wrong side and tack it in place. Turn in the raw edges of the handle $\frac{3}{4}''$ and then fold them over again to touch at the centre. Tack in position. Oversew (overcast) this seam and then machine stitch down both edges of the handle $\frac{1}{4}''$ from the edge.

7 Pin the handle on the inside of the bag at the side seams. Each end of the handle should extend $\frac{3}{4}''$ beyond the $1\frac{3}{4}''$ hem at the top of the bag. Sew both ends of the handle in place very securely as most of the weight is taken at these two points. Remove all tacking stitches.

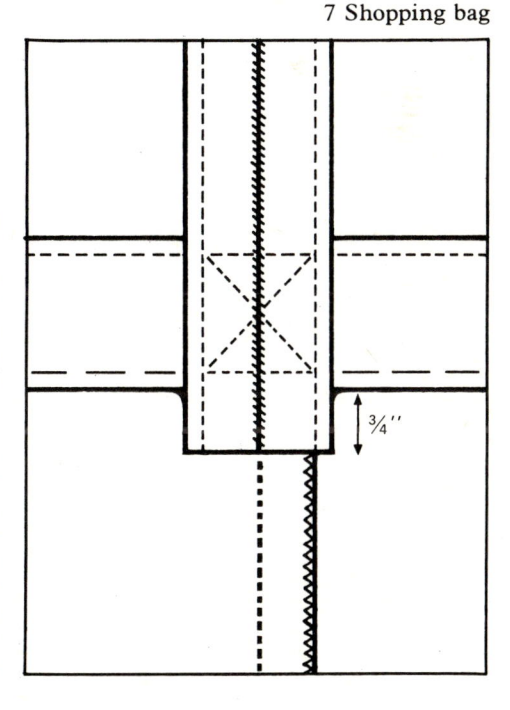

7 Shopping bag

Shopping bag

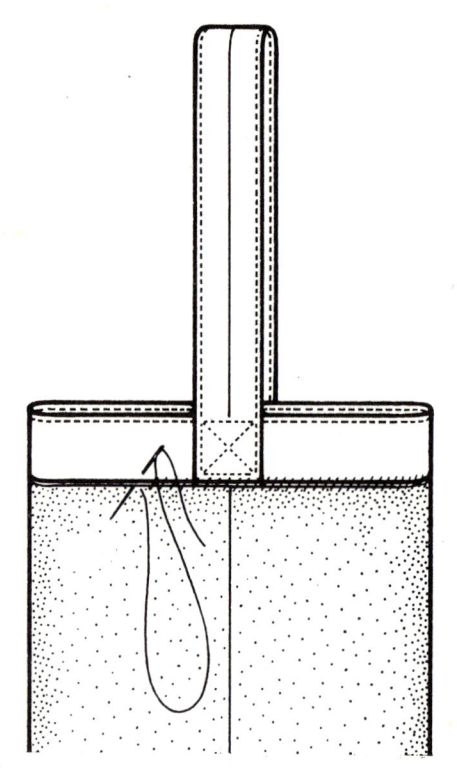

8 Shopping bag

9 For the fringe at the base of the bag cut thirty 10" lengths of mauve ribbon, cutting the ends diagonally to prevent fraying. Fold each ribbon in half and thread the loops along the bottom of the bag at $\frac{1}{2}$" intervals. Draw the ribbon ends through the loops and pull up tightly.

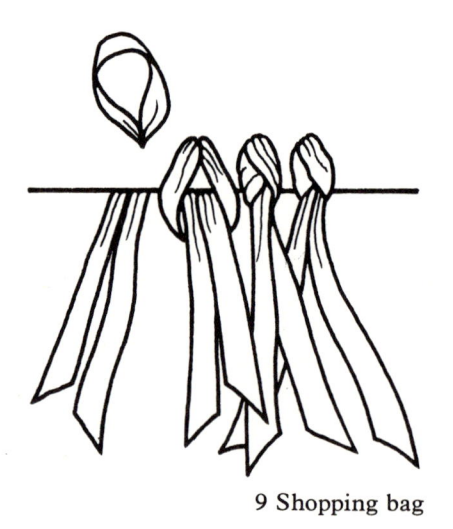

9 Shopping bag

10 Shopping bag

8 Make the lining by folding the piece of strong cotton in half widthwise and sew down the side and along the bottom allowing a $\frac{1}{2}$" seam. Turn the lining the right way out (so that the seams are on the inside), and turn under a $\frac{1}{2}$" hem at the top and secure with tacking stitch. Pull the lining over the bag (still inside out), aligning the side seams of the bag with the side seam and centre fold of the lining, and pin it to the hem at the top of the bag. Stitch the top of the bag and the lining together securely, taking the sewing thread through to the front of the bag so that the hem at the top is held in place. Remove all tacking stitches.

10 When they are all in place, knot adjacent ends of adjacent ribbons together in tight reef knots. To prevent the fringe sticking out in all directions, it is advisable to iron it.

Metric conversion table

inches	centimetres	yards	metres
⅛	0.3	¼	0.2
¼	0.6	½	0.4
½	1.3	¾	0.7
¾	1.9		
		1	0.9
1	2.5	2	1.8
2	5.0	3	2.7
3	7.6	4	3.7
4	10.2	5	4.6
5	12.7		
		6	5.5
6	15.2	7	6.4
7	17.8	8	7.3
8	20.3	9	8.2
9	22.9	10	9.1
10	25.4		
20	50.8		
30	76.2		
40	101.6		

If measurements in between those listed are wanted, simply add together the two component parts. For example, 1½″ equals 1″ plus ½″, which from the table is 2.5 plus 1.3 centimetres, ie 3.8 centimetres; or 36″ equals 30″ plus 6″, which from the table is 76.2 plus 15.2 centimetres, ie 91.4 centimetres.

Some useful relationships are:
1 metre = 100 centimetres

¼ yard = 9″
½ yard = 18″
¾ yard = 27″
1 yard = 36″